Langenscheidt

The Gunpowder Plot

by Alan Broude

Langenscheidt

Berlin · München · Wien · Zürich · New York

Übungen von Carole Eilertson
Muttersprachliche Durchsicht: Charlotte Collins
Lektorat: Momo Evers
Coverfoto: Nancy Glor

Umwelthinweis: Gedruckt auf chlorfrei gebleichtem Papier

www.langenscheidt.de

ISBN-13: 978-3-468-44103-5
ISBN-10: 3-468-44103-7

1. 2. 3. 4. 5. • 11 10 09 08 07

Remember, remember the fifth of November,
Gunpowder, **treason** and plot.
I see no reason why gunpowder treason
Should ever be forgot.
—17th century children's rhyme

In 1604 a group of English Catholics began planning a coup against the government of King James I. They had hoped for greater tolerance from the new king, whose queen was herself a Catholic, as his mother had been. The previous English monarch, Queen Elizabeth, **had** severely **penalized** practising Catholics; the Jesuit order in particular was targeted as its high standards of education and loyalty to the Pope were seen as a political threat. However, James instead reconfirmed Elizabeth's anti-Catholic **legislation**; he also ended England's war with Spain, removing any hope of **imposing** Catholicism by force.
The thirteen coup plotters had intended to blow up the House of Lords on the day that Parliament **convened**, killing the king in the process. Guy Fawkes, who had fought for Spain as a **mercenary**, would light the **fuse** and then flee to Spain, while Robert Catesby, the leader of the plot, would raise a rebellion among Catholics in the north of England.

---

treason [ˈtriːzn] (Landes-)Verrat **to penalize** [ˈpiːnəlaɪz] bestrafen **legislation** [ˌledʒɪsˈleɪʃn] Gesetzgebung **to impose** [ɪmˈpəʊz] durchsetzen **to convene** [kənˈviːn] sich versammeln **mercenary** [ˈmɜːsənərɪ] Söldner **fuse** [fjuːz] Zünder

The **Gunpowder Plot remains deeply ingrained** in the collective British **consciousness.** 'Guy Fawkes Night' is still **commemorated** every year on November 5th in villages, towns, and cities across England with large bonfires and the burning of a straw man representing Fawkes. The full truth behind the Plot, however, has never been uncovered.

—Sebekova, K.: The History of Britain. London 2031

Gunpowder Plot ['gʌnpaʊdə plɒt] *wörtl.:* ‚Pulververschwörung' **to remain deeply ingrained** [rɪˌmeɪn 'diːplɪ ɪnˌgreɪnd] tief verwurzelt sein **consciousness** ['kɒnʃəsnəs] Bewusstsein **to commemorate** [kə'meməreɪt] eine Gedenkfeier abhalten für

One

Professor Anthony Johnson **shuffled** slowly around the **lecture theatre**, carefully examining each of the fresh-faced students before him. Twenty-seven pairs of eyes avoided his stare as he moved silently between the wooden desks, pausing occasionally behind a random student for a few moments of quiet **intimidation**. Britain's brightest young minds **fidgeted** nervously **with** their pens, half-afraid that their eccentric teacher would attack them at any moment.

As Johnson moved quietly back towards the top of the oval, wood-panelled room, he folded his hands casually behind his back, making the brown leather patches on the elbows of his tweed jacket stand out like the wide eyes of a **praying mantis**. Out of the corner of his eye he could see the students raising their eyebrows as if quietly confirming to one another that their new professor was indeed quite mad. With his back to the class, Johnson peered out over the half-moon spectacles that perched **precariously** on the end of his long, thin nose. Ignoring the pached lecture hall behind him, he studied the gold-framed print of Vermeer's *The Allegory of Painting*, which he had placed in the centre of the wall behind his desk. Tipping his head slowly backwards, he stroked his greying **goatee**, displaying to the class the bald patch on the top of his head. He gazed up at the portrait of Clio, the Greek muse of History, with her blue

---

to shuffle ['ʃʌfl] schlurfen **lecture theatre** ['lektʃə ˌθɪətə] Hörsaal **intimidation** [ɪnˌtɪmɪ'deɪʃn] Einschüchterung **to fidget with sth.** ['fɪdʒɪt wɪð] mit etw. herumspielen **praying mantis** [ˌpreɪɪŋ 'mæntɪs] Gottesanbeterin **precariously** [prɪ'keərɪəslɪ] *hier:* abenteuerlich **goatee** [gəʊ'tiː] Spitzbart

dress, feather-decorated hair, her eyes lowered in the direction of the large book she held to her breast; and suddenly he broke the silence.

"FOOLS," he boomed at the top of his voice, turning quickly on his heels and **glaring at** the class, "will tell you that the study of History is little more than a luxurious **pastime** for those who can afford not to work!" He took a step forward, his large green eyes **bulging** as they scanned the room and finally came to rest on a young girl, trembling with regret at having taken a seat in the front row. "FOOLS," he cried again, pointing a skeletal finger at the door as if the forces of darkness were at that moment gathering great armies in an unholy war against him, "will tell you that the discipline of History can never be a *real* science!"

He was nodding his head repeatedly now, helpfully confirming the truth of this revelation. "FOOLS will tell you that historians can never be *ob-jec-tive*!" He whispered this last word softly as though it offended him to speak it. "If any of you agree with these sentiments, you can get out now." The professor looked around the room, pausing to allow the students a moment to consider. "Go on! Go off and study flower-arranging or basket-weaving or **tap-dancing** or whatever the hell you like!"

Johnson gained immense pleasure from **inflicting** this micro-drama **on** his new students every September. Judging from their expressions, he felt he might now be ready for a career on the stage.

---

to glare at sth. ['gleə ət] etw. wütend anstarren **pastime** 'pɑːstaɪm] Zeitvertreib **to bulge** [bʌldʒ] sich wölben **tap-dancing** ['tæpˌdɑːnsɪŋ] Stepptanz **to inflict sth. on sb.** [ɪn'flɪkt / ɒn] *hier:* etw. über jmdn. hernieder gehen lassen

"How many of you," he asked, "will become true historians? Which of you will discover the secret to understanding the past? Who amongst you … "

He knew his motivational speech by heart and was able **to rattle** it **off** like a prayer learned in childhood, allowing his mind to wander onto simpler things, such as how the students seemed to grow younger by the year. It was extraordinary, he thought, that most of the first years sitting before him were little more than **impure** intentions in the minds of their parents when he had studied History here at Oxford in the early 2020s.

"Of those of you who decide to stay in this class, most of you will perform adequately. Some of you will do respectably well. And we may even **unearth** one or two independent thinkers amongst you. What is quite certain, however, is that there will be a few of you for whom the only history you will study this year will be the paintings on the walls of the King's Arms pub in Hollywell Street."

The students **emitted** a collective nervous laugh as the professor playfully **scowled at** an unshaven youth with greasy hair and tired red eyes.

The first day of the new academic year was always Johnson's favourite; he **relished** the challenge of winning over the students with his eccentric charm and **intimidating** passion. He loved the possibilities that the first day held – the knowledge that he would meet a couple of outstanding

---

to rattle sth. off [ˌrætl / ˈɒf] etw. herunterrattern **impure** [ɪmˈpjʊə] schmutzig **to unearth** [ʌnˈɜːθ] ans Licht bringen **to emit** [ɪˈmɪt] ausstoßen **to scowl at sb.** [ˈskaʊl ət] jmdn. finster anschauen **to relish** [ˈrelɪʃ] genießen **intimidating** [ɪnˈtɪmɪdeɪtɪŋ] einschüchternd

new students, the chance to persuade a few others of the value of studying History, and the opportunity to make his classes more engaging. He wondered whether any of the young faces sitting in front of him would one day change history themselves. Oxford had produced countless presidents, prime ministers, and Nobel prize winners; Johnson thought it a **grave** injustice that there was no Nobel Prize for History, and regularly encouraged his students to start an annual protest outside the Concert Hall in Stockholm.

The professor was passionate about his subject. He was irritated by what he called 'these annoying presentists' – people who believe that the time in which they live is somehow deeply significant in the history of humanity, that only their generation has been confronted with monumental, **unprecedented** challenges. "How," Johnson asked the class, "can we possibly judge the importance of our own era if we cannot accurately compare it against all other times?"

As the professor continued his monologue, he caught a brief glimpse of a woman in black peering in through the glass **pane** of the lecture theatre door. She smiled at him, nodded a silent greeting and then disappeared from view.

When the students eventually filed out of the room, Johnson began to gather up his papers and books and put them **haphazardly** into his battered leather satchel. As he struggled to turn off the digital monitor – he had a natural **aversion** to all things technological – he was startled by a voice from just behind him.

"Professor Johnson."

---

grave [greɪv] schwerwiegend **unprecedented** [ʌnˈpresɪdentɪd] beispiellos **pane** [peɪn] Scheibe **haphazardly** [hæpˈhæzədlɪ] willkürlich **aversion** [əˈvɜːʃn] Abscheu

Exercise 1: Are the following statements true or false? Mark each box with either a "T" or an "F".

1. ☐ Professor Anthony Johnson enjoys teasing his students.
2. ☐ Johnson studied History at Oxford in the late 2010s.
3. ☐ Johnson's biggest ambition is to join the ranks of Nobel prize winners.
4. ☐ Johnson is enthusiastic about his chosen subject.
5. ☐ Johnson's regular place of work is an operation theatre.
6. ☐ Johnson is in his mid-twenties.
7. ☐ The room is oval-shaped with wood panels.
8. ☐ Johnson's hobbies include tap-dancing and basket-weaving.
9. ☐ Johnson prefers to avoid new technology.
10. ☐ Johnson expects that most of his pupils will be independent thinkers.

"Yes?" Johnson turned to see a woman standing before him with thick white hair styled in a **pageboy cut** which hung to her shoulders. He judged her age to be somewhere around seventy, from the crow's feet around her **piercing** blue eyes; they were kind and sincere, reminding him at once of his grandmother, with whom he had lived as a child.
"That was quite a performance," she said with a slight smile, as if suggesting that they were both part of a successful **conspiracy** against the students. "For a moment I wondered whether you were teaching History or Drama."

---

pageboy (hair)cut ['peɪdʒbɔɪ ˌheəkʌt] Pagenkopf **piercing** ['pɪəsɪŋ] durchdringend **conspiracy** [kən'spɪrəsɪ] Verschwörung

"Thank you," replied Johnson, **flattered** by the compliment but still waiting for an explanation as to who she was and why she was there.
"Do you believe everything you told them?"
Although her smile remained, Johnson was unsettled at how she pressed the conversation without engaging in the usual introductory formalities. It was a little rude, he thought; but he went along with it, for now, without protest. "Yes, of course I do," he replied, adopting a more formal tone in response to her slight and unexpected arrogance.
"You believe that history can be truly objective?"
"Yes, I … I'm sorry, have we … ?"
"No, Professor. We haven't met before."
Johnson thought she was about to explain herself. He was wrong.
"How can history be objective when we rarely have all the facts at our disposal?"
An ***imperious*** *old dame*, he thought, feeling increasingly annoyed by her persistence. He returned his attention to packing his things, annoyed with himself that he was unable to meet her penetrating stare. "We have records. We have ancient books and texts. We have memoirs written by important figures and the diaries of ordinary people. We have illustrations, art, and architecture. We have oral histories. We have surviving rituals and traditions. We have **retrospective** tests that can evaluate related hypotheses. We can use all these to assemble a fairly accurate picture of the key historical events and trends, can't we?"

---

to be flattered [biː ˈflætəd] geschmeichelt sein **imperious** [ɪmˈpɪərɪəs] herrisch **retrospective** [ˌretrəˈspektɪv] rückblickend

"Perhaps, but these records are human records. Humans tend to exaggerate, don't they? Humans are **fallible** – people lie, facts become **distorted**, memories become selective, and accuracy is too often **abandoned** in favour of the dramatic. And even if we confirm the authenticity of certain facts, how can we be sure that our interpretation of them isn't coloured by our own beliefs and values?"

Johnson was finding it increasingly difficult to hide his annoyance. Who was she to come in here like this and raise such questions without even the **courtesy** of a proper introduction? "Forgive me, but when you have studied History for a considerable period of time, you begin to understand that your own beliefs and values, whatever they may be, are rarely strong enough to obstruct the truth."

"Ah, the *truth*. What you are saying then, Professor, is that even if we could go back into the past and observe great historical events as they happened, we would add no more to our understanding of history, that we wouldn't increase our knowledge?"

"That's a different matter entirely. There are things we don't know about the past, of course. That is a simple absence of factual information. What I am saying is that we can be objective about the things that we *do* know. If we could observe historical events at first hand, then of course we could answer some very important questions." Johnson paused for a moment.

The **conspiratorial** smile had returned to the woman's face. "We can," she said.

---

fallible ['fæləbl] fehlbar **distorted** [dɪ'stɔːtɪd] verzerrt **to be abandoned** [biː ə'bændənd] aufgeben werden **courtesy** ['kɜːtəsɪ] Höflichkeit **conspiratorial** [kənˌspɪrə'tɔːrɪəl] verschwörerisch

"We can *what*?" asked Johnson, no longer hiding his irritation.
"We can 'observe historical events at first hand', as you describe it."
Johnson released a deep sigh, intended to suggest that her mysterious manner was becoming **tiresome**, if she was not prepared to be clear about her intentions. "Forgive me, Mrs …?"
"Smith."
"Forgive me, Mrs Smith, I don't want to sound rude, but who are you exactly, and is there perhaps something specific I can help you with? I sense that you did not come here to debate my academic discipline with me."
"Professor Johnson, there is something I would like to show you that would be of **immeasurable** interest to a person such as yourself. After you have seen it, you may even question the existence of God and the certainty of your own place in the universe. Nothing will appear the same to you again. Time, space, reality, truth – the very foundations on which your world is built – will be turned inside out and upside down."
"Now there you go again, Mrs Smith, speaking in riddles. How can you expect me to react if you don't clearly … "
"I'll explain everything in the car, Professor."
Before Johnson could respond, she had turned and left the lecture theatre. The professor grabbed his satchel and overcoat, holding them clumsily to his chest as he ran after her. Although she **was** twenty years **his senior**, Smith was halfway down the corridor by the time he had left the theatre.

---

tiresome ['taɪəsəm] lästig **immeasurable** [ɪ'meʒərəbl] unermesslich **to be sb.'s senior** [bi: / 'si:nɪə] älter als jmd. sein

"Excuse me! Mrs Smith! *Excuse me!*"

Mrs Smith stopped and turned, smiling at Johnson who now felt like a walrus out of water as he bounded down the corridor after her.

When they left the college, Johnson followed Mrs Smith into the back of a dark Jaguar with blacked-out windows and a solid screen separating them from the driver. He couldn't see where they were going, but he knew Oxford intimately and from the sequence of sharp turns they took he could sense that they were heading east. When they had left the city and joined the motorway traffic, Mrs Smith finally spoke.

"Professor Johnson. What I am about to tell you is the most **closely-guarded** secret in Britain today, perhaps in the world. All your instincts will tell you that it is not true. That is not important now – you will see the evidence of it when we reach our destination. For now, I simply want you to pay attention."

"Yes, of course," Johnson replied, feeling that, quite without warning, his role had changed from teacher to student.

"Twenty-seven years ago, after China defeated Britain and our allies in the Taiwan War, the Ministry of Defence received the largest budget increase in its history. The money was never accounted for publicly, and appeared on no official budget. Much of it came from the private sector, particularly from leading arms manufacturers. The project was so secret that even most Cabinet ministers were unaware of it. After all, politicians are out of power within a few years, and this project was expected to take much

---

closely-guarded [ˌkləʊslɪˈɡɑːdɪd] streng bewacht

longer than the **duration** of a political career. In the end, it took decades. You see, Professor, Western leaders were deeply traumatized by their loss against China – much more so than the public realized at the time. Many of them simply could not accept the reality of what had happened and they became obsessed with analysing what had gone wrong. They kept asking themselves pointless questions: 'Why did we not believe the Chinese would act on their threats? What if we had acted earlier? What could we have done differently?' But what began as a relatively harmless exercise in **counterfactual** speculation quickly evolved into a radical and obsessive political objective – to change the past."

"You mean to **revise** the history books, to reinterpret events?"

"No, Professor. I mean they wanted to physically travel back in time and launch a **pre-emptive strike** on China in order to change the outcome of the war."

"But that's **insane**!"

"Insane? Maybe. Foolish? Certainly. Possible? We didn't think so. Unfortunately, the politicians failed to understand the complexity of their request. They thought that any problem could be solved as long as they threw enough money at it. Perhaps mercifully, we were completely unsuccessful for a very long time. As the years passed, relations with China improved, old leaders gave way to a new generation who had come to terms with the past, and once again, trade and diplomacy replaced military aggression.

---

duration [djʊˈreɪʃn] Dauer **counterfactual** [ˈkaʊntəˌfæktʃʊəl] hypothetisch **to revise** [rɪˈvaɪz] überarbeiten **pre-emptive strike** [prɪˌemptɪv ˈstraɪk] Präventivschlag **insane** [ɪnˈseɪn] verrückt

But the project continued. Nine years ago, in September 2046, Dr Peter Fanshawe, our chief scientist, was responsible for perhaps the greatest achievement in the history of physics – he managed to build a device that successfully produced closed time-like curves."

"Closed what?"

"Closed time-like curves, Professor. Space-time **trajectories** that are bent into loops, allowing us to move to points in the past without ever having to exceed the speed of light. The theory had been around since the 1980s but almost no one believed it could ever be turned into a reality. Six years after Dr Fanshawe proved them wrong, when we were confident that everything was ready, we sent a mouse into the past. We strapped a miniature camera to his head and he returned with images from the year 1972. Within a year, we had sent our first human back a hundred years. It is the policy of our present Prime Minister that this technology should not be used to change history, only to understand it better. She is a very wise woman, for a politician. Last year, she **expanded** our **mandate** and established the Department of Historical Truth in order to pursue this goal. As you might expect, only the Prime Minister, one or two senior civil servants, and our staff know of its existence. As a general rule we believe that secrecy in government is unnecessary and counterproductive, but this technology presents profound new challenges. Can you imagine the **havoc** that might result if it were to fall into the wrong hands?"

Johnson nodded enthusiastically, despite having no idea

---

trajectory [trəˈdʒektərɪ] Flugbahn **to expand a mandate** [ɪkˌspænd ə ˈmændeɪt] ein Mandat erweitern **havoc** [ˈhævək] Chaos

what the consequences might be if the public were made aware of the technology; his head was **giddy** with the information and it was taking all his mental energy just to absorb what Smith was telling him.

"We have been instructed to concentrate on key turning points in history, beginning, of course, at home in Britain. We want to focus on those events and trends that have had the most profound effects on our country, particularly on the internal political dynamics that have led to major economic, social and cultural **shifts.** This is where you come in."

Exercise 2: Put these statements into *chronological* order, according to the events in the story.

a. ☐ Dr Peter Fanshawe invented a time travel device.
b. ☐ Johnson and the mysterious woman in black drove east.
c. ☐ The Ministry of Defence received a budget increase.
d. ☐ A mouse was sent back into the past with a camera strapped to its back.
e. ☐ An elderly woman approached Johnson.
f. ☐ A human being was sent back one hundred years in time.
g. ☐ China defeated Britain and her allies in the Taiwan War.
h. ☐ The Prime Minister established the Department of Historical Truth.

Johnson knew that Mrs Smith had paused to allow him to react, but he found himself incapable of putting a **coherent**

---

giddy ['gɪdɪ] schwindelig **shift** [ʃɪft] Umstrukturierung **coherent** [kəʊ'hɪərənt] zusammenhängend

thought together. An hour ago he had carried off a masterful performance of **eloquence** and knowledge; now he couldn't even have said his name if he had been asked. Random images of major historical events passed before his mind's eye – the Roman occupation, the arrival of the Germanic tribes and the Vikings, the development of the English language, the Crusades, the Black Death, the Reformation of the Church, the defeat of the Spanish **Armada**, the **beheading** of Mary, Queen of Scots, and later of King Charles I, the Civil War, the Great Fire of London, the Industrial Revolution, the rise and fall of the British Empire, three world wars … He had a thousand questions to ask Smith. He started with the most obvious: "Why me?"
"Our staff members, Professor, are physicists. You are a historian. We need both. The reputation that you have on the early seventeenth century is **unparalleled**. Your strong belief in the necessity of adopting a scientific approach to history **has endeared** you **to** the Prime Minister, and, for what it's worth, to me. You are the perfect person to help us uncover the truth about the plot."
As Johnson **shifted** uncomfortably on the leather seat, he loosened his tie, undid the top button of his shirt, and quietly asked, "What plot?"
Smith stared at him without blinking for what seemed an eternity.
"The Gunpowder Plot, Professor Johnson."

---

eloquence ['eləkwəns] Beredsamkeit **armada** [ɑː'mɑːdə] Kriegsflotte **beheading** [bɪ'hedɪŋ] Enthauptung **unparalleled** [ʌn'pærəleld] ohnegleichen **to endear o.s. to sb.** [ɪn'dɪə / tə] sich bei jmdm. beliebt machen **to shift** [ʃɪft] sich (unruhig) bewegen

Two

The car came to a stop outside a large farmhouse in the countryside, several kilometres from the nearest main road and hidden from view by a tightly packed **cluster** of tall **elm trees**. When the two back doors opened simultaneously, Smith nodded, indicating that they had reached their destination. As the car sped off, Johnson followed Smith towards a large hay barn behind the house. They went inside, walking past old tools, rusting farm machinery, and bales of hay piled up to the roof. In the far back corner, behind an old-fashioned **manure spreader**, Smith stopped and pointed at an iron handle in the ground. "Professor, would you mind opening that, please?"

He bent down and pulled the handle towards him. It opened a small trapdoor, from which a small amount of light spilled into the barn. Smith smiled as she nodded towards the staircase that descended into the earth. Johnson went first, turning to help Smith who quickly shook her head. "I've been walking up and down these stairs without help for twenty-seven years, Professor. But thank you **all the same**."

At the foot of the staircase Johnson found himself standing in front of a large black wall. Smith moved past him and stood perfectly still until a thin blue light shot out and connected with her right eye. As soon as it disappeared, a voice spoke: "Good evening, Smith. Your password, please."

"Truth," she said, glancing at Johnson with a **wry** smile as if

---

cluster ['klʌstə] Gruppe **elm (tree)** ['elm triː] Ulme **manure spreader** [mə'njʊə ˌspredə] Düngerstreumaschine **all the same** [ˌɔːl ðə 'seɪm] trotzdem **wry** [raɪ] ironisch

reminding him of their earlier conversation. The wall quickly separated into two parts, allowing just enough space for both of them to pass. Johnson walked through behind Smith, and found himself suspended on a metal platform overlooking a large, kidney-shaped room. Seven people dressed in black and silver suits looked up, acknowledged them both, and then returned their attention to a rectangular glass panel hanging from the ceiling. Red lights flickered above four-digit numbers that stretched the length of the panel – 1776, 1789, 1798, 1800, 1856, 1874, 1888, 1900, 1914, 1939, 1962, 1968, 1989, 1991, 2001, 2008, 2019, 2031.

"Professor Johnson, welcome to the Department of Historical Truth. If you decide to assist us, this room will become very familiar to you over the next few months."

For a brief moment, Johnson wondered what might happen if he decided not to assist them. Would they simply let him leave, having seen and learned so much? He thought that they must have been very confident that he would agree before bringing him to this place.

Smith gave the professor a tour of the **facility**, explaining in a little more detail the theory behind time travel and how it worked in practice. As she was speaking, a **portly** middle-aged man with a thick black moustache that entirely covered his upper lip approached them on the platform. The friendly smile that shifted his **chubby cheeks** high enough to make him **squint** couldn't prevent Johnson from focussing instead on a **wisp** of black hair that flowed behind him

---

facility [fəˈsɪlətɪ] Anlage **portly** [ˈpɔːtlɪ] wohlbeleibt **chubby** [ˈtʃʌbɪ] pausbäckig **cheek** [tʃiːk] Wange **to squint** [skwɪnt] schielen **wisp** [wɪsp] Strähne

like a loyal pet as if it were **chasing**, rather than attached to, his **balding** head. He wore a traditional long white coat over a three-piece suit.
"If you are really interested, this man can tell you exactly how it all works. Professor Johnson, this is Dr Peter Fanshawe, or, as he prefers to be called, God."
Johnson's first impression of Fanshawe was of an affectionate and sensitive man who had the kind of lengthy and sincere handshake that would endear him to some and scare others away. It would normally have been a little over-enthusiastic for Johnson, but these were exceptional circumstances. Johnson spotted a gold chain strung across the front of Fanshawe's suit and assumed it was attached to an antique watch in the pocket of his waistcoat. "Are you a collector, Dr Fanshawe?" he said, pointing at the chain.
"Well, time is my business, Professor, so yes, I think it's fair to say that I'm a collector – watches, clocks, **sundials**, calendars, I collect them all! And now, with this little project we're running here, I suppose you could say I'm collecting time itself!" Fanshawe gave a sudden snort as if **belatedly** recognizing the wit in his own comment. As Smith rolled her eyes to heaven, Johnson smiled politely, thinking that Fanshawe may indeed be a genius, but that his repertoire of talents certainly didn't extend to comedy. As the three of them walked the length of the platform towards Smith's office, Johnson looked over the railing and saw a large glass tube ten metres below that reminded him of the long walkway between terminals six and seven at Heathrow Airport. Blue lights rippled along the top of the tube and a

---

to chase [tʃeɪs] jagen **balding** [ˈbɑːldɪŋ] kahl werdend **sundial** [ˈsʌnˌdaɪəl] Sonnenuhr **belatedly** [bɪˈleɪtɪdlɪ] verspätet

heavy electronic **drone** spilled out in slow waves. They paused to watch as a man dressed in nineteenth century clothing stood at the front of the tube. Fanshawe handed them both a **pair of goggles** as a light behind the man became increasingly intense. Then, suddenly, the man disappeared. There was no noise, no fanfare, no excitement. Fanshawe nudged Johnson, grinning and pointing as if they had balcony seats at a West End show. For a few brief seconds, the red light flickering above the number 1888 changed to green. They both turned their attention from the glass panel to the far end of the tube where the same man was now standing. "I know who he is!" the man shouted as he came back to the main room on a **conveyor belt** parallel to the time tube.

Johnson turned to Fanshawe, a look of confusion spreading across his face. "He knows who *who* is?"

"Jack the Ripper. We watched this man leave and return in an instant, but he has just spent two months of his life living in London in the year 1888."

"That's impossible!" said Johnson, stepping back from the railing. "That's simply not *possible.*"

Before he could take in the **implications** of what he had just seen, Smith led him into her office with Fanshawe **trailing behind**, still **sporting** a child-like grin from ear to ear, the lights in the office reflecting off his red cheeks. Johnson was surprised at how small the room was; he would have expected the Head of the Department to have

---

drone [drəʊn] Dröhnen **pair of goggles** [peə' əv 'gɒglz] Schutzbrille **conveyor belt** [kən'veɪə belt] Fließband **implication** [ˌɪmplɪ'keɪʃn] Bedeutung **to trail behind** [ˌtreɪl bɪ'haɪnd] nachfolgen **to sport** [spɔːt] (stolz) tragen

had an office **befitting** the seniority and importance of her post. Instead he found himself in a modest room with just enough space for a narrow bookshelf, an old-fashioned **filing cabinet**, two guest chairs, and a small desk, behind which Smith now sat. The wall to Smith's left was made entirely of glass, allowing her to supervise the activity in the main room below. A grandfather clock hung on the wall to her right; when Johnson realized that the time was wrong he took a closer look and saw that all the hands were moving backwards.

Exercise 3: Which words go together? Find the appropriate pairs.

1.	child-like	☐ **a.**	midriff
2.	balding	☐ **b.**	Revolution
3.	cube-shaped	☐ **c.**	cheeks
4.	filing	☐ **d.**	grin
5.	expanding	☐ **e.**	room
6.	Gunpowder	☐ **f.**	clothing
7.	sincere	☐ **g.**	cabinet
8.	seventeenth-century	☐ **h.**	handshake
9.	Industrial	☐ **i.**	Plot
10.	chubby	☐ **j.**	head

As they settled down, Johnson noticed a **brass plate mounted** on the wall behind Smith's desk. From the corner of his eye, he could see that Smith was pleased he had noticed it. As she slowly read out the three words with just the

---

to befit [bɪˈfɪt] angemessen sein **filing cabinet** [ˈfaɪlɪŋ ˌkæbɪnət] Aktenschrank **brass plate** [ˈbrɑːs pleɪt] Messingschild **mounted** [ˈmaʊntɪd] montiert

slightest hint of **condescension** in her voice, her tone suggested that she was both taking pity on his poor eyesight and challenging him to translate the Latin text at the same time. "*Veritas temporis filia*, Professor."

"Ah! Truth is the daughter of Time."

"She is, indeed; and so we find ourselves in the role of parents, with hopes and dreams for our child, but also with profound responsibilities. To date, we have been successful beyond imagining; everything that we have set out to achieve has been completed. Everyone who has been sent into the past has returned **unharmed**. Our operation remains a secret, and we are in the process of building substantially on our knowledge of history. However, we have not yet sent anyone back further than the late eighteenth century, nor for longer than three months. Perhaps most importantly, none of our investigators has interacted with anyone in the past. They have kept as much distance as possible from others and carried out all their observations discreetly. We are now confident that we can go back further in time, and for longer periods. Dr Fanshawe has expressed a strong desire to join you on this project, if you should choose to accept it. And as he has **painstakingly** described the technology to other scientists, we can now take the risk that he may not return. We are sending him, however, not because of his personal desire to experience time travel, but because of his technical knowledge."

Fanshawe smiled, doing his best to look appreciative and **humble**. He then turned to speak directly to Johnson. "It's

---

condescension [ˌkɒndɪˈsenʃn] Herablassung **unharmed** ˌʌnˈhɑːmd] unversehrt **painstakingly** [ˈpeɪnzˌteɪkɪŋlɪ] sorgfältig **humble** [ˈhʌmbl] bescheiden

true – we haven't the slightest idea about the implications of travelling back so far and for such a long period!" Fanshawe said this with a beaming smile that suggested this **crucial** gap in knowledge was something of a bonus, an **unpredictable** element that offered exciting opportunities for scientific discovery, rather than a terrifying **admission** that they might not return at all. "Even now, even after all our successes, we still **haven't resolved** many of the paradoxes of time travel. We might not even be aware of them all! We know that it works, but we don't know whether we **will encounter** some **constraints** that the laws of physics will not allow, and if this happens, we haven't got a clue what the implications might be for our investigators! As yet we have no **conclusive** evidence of the effects of time travel on a person's age, for example."

Fanshawe's smile widened as he shifted his weight, seemingly unaware of his own **discomfort** in the narrow seat as he became more excited about the limits of his own knowledge. "We're also not sure what would happen if someone were to die in the past. Would that mean that they would never be born in the future? If so, they would never have had the opportunity to travel back to the past in the first place and so couldn't die there. Does the future perhaps **overrule** the past? If someone dies in the past, does this simply negate their presence there, returning them to the

---

crucial ['kruːʃl] entscheidend **unpredictable** [ˌʌnprɪ'dɪktəbl] unberechenbar **admission** [əd'mɪʃn] Eingeständnis **to resolve** [rɪ'zɒlv] lösen **to encounter** [ɪn'kaʊntə] begegnen **constraint** [kən'streɪnt] Beschränkung **conclusive** [kən'kluːsɪv] schlüssig **discomfort** [dɪs'kʌmfət] Unbehagen **to overrule sth.** [ˌəʊvə'ruːl] über etw. die Oberhand gewinnen

original point of departure? **We haven't got a clue**! A few months ago, we injected some **mice** with slow-acting poison, and then sent them into the past, making sure that they would die before returning."

His smile faded quickly. "Unfortunately, the results so far have been **inconclusive**."

Johnson leaned back in his chair, and rubbed his eyes. He was overwhelmed at what he had seen and heard, and struggled to concentrate as Smith began to speak again.

"Theoretical questions aside, we have no intention of creating the world's first time martyrs. Your safety is of the highest importance, and your training will focus on this. Professor, earlier I mentioned the Gunpowder Plot. As you know, Henry VIII **severed** links with Rome in 1533 in order to divorce his first wife who could not bear him a male **heir**. From that point on, Catholics in this country were in grave danger; monasteries were burnt to the ground and priests went into hiding for fear of their lives. Had Guy Fawkes not been caught on the fourth of November 1605, things may have turned out differently; but of course, the failure of the plot led to even greater **persecution** of Catholics under King James I. Those people who refused to attend Protestant church services were **humiliated**, fined, imprisoned, tortured, and **slaughtered** for another two centuries. Whatever the consequences were, and however much we speculate on what might have happened had the

---

We haven't got a clue. [wɪ 'hævnt gɒt ə 'kluː] Wir haben keine Ahnung. **mouse (*pl.* mice)** [maʊs / maɪs] Maus **inconclusive** [ˌɪnkən'kluːsɪv] nicht schlüssig **to sever** ['sevə] abbrechen **heir** [eə] Erbe **persecution** [ˌpɜːsɪ'kjuːʃn] Verfolgung **to be humiliated** [biː hjuː'mɪlɪeɪtɪd] gedemütigt werden **to slaughter** ['slɔːtə] abschlachten

plot been successful, the truth is that we still don't know the details of what actually took place. We don't know for certain that the entire plot wasn't a conspiracy by James's chief minister Robert Cecil, and if it wasn't, we don't know for sure who wrote the infamous letter to Lord Monteagle warning him of the plot in advance, or even if the letter was authentic. I'm sure you'll agree that this represents a major gap in our national history. I should also add that one of the Department's objectives is to confirm what we think we *do* know."

"A wise idea."

"I'm glad you agree. Professor, if you choose to help us, you will not only be providing a great service to your country, you will also be the first non-state employee in the world to undertake time travel. As a History professor, this is obviously the kind of opportunity that you must have dreamed about but never imagined possible. However, just as Dr Fanshawe will never receive a **knighthood** or the Nobel Prize for Physics, you will never publish an academic article or book about your new research. You will never be able to speak about it to anyone, including your colleagues and students. This will be very difficult for you, but we will help you to deal with it."

"Thank you." Johnson was at a complete loss for something sensible to say in the middle of such a surreal conversation.

"Although we can send you there and back in an instant, we cannot send you immediately. We will need to prepare you for life in the early seventeenth century. You will have to study the **mannerisms**, practices, and social etiquette of

---

knighthood ['naɪthʊd] Rittertum **mannerism** ['mænərɪzm] Eigenarten

the time in order to fit in without being noticed. You will have to learn to speak with a seventeenth century accent and dialect. It will be stressful living under these conditions, and you will need to be physically and mentally strong – essentially, you will be living a lie for the duration of your trip. You will take intensive classes in acting and improvisation – most of this will take place under conditions of simulated reality where you will interact with computer-generated characters from the period. Perhaps most importantly, you will be trained in emotional **detachment**. It is crucial that you do not form close, personal relationships with the people you meet in the past. This could severely **impair** your judgement and prevent you from maintaining an objective viewpoint. We will send you back to May 1604, eighteen months before the plot was uncovered. We want you to study the entire process from beginning to end. I realize that this is a considerable period of time and a massive **undertaking**, but I need to know now, Professor, whether you are interested in this mission."

Exercise 4: Put the following sentences into the passive voice, e.g. Dr Fanshawe described the technology. *The technology was described.*

1. The laws of physics limit time-travel.

____

2. We haven't resolved some of the paradoxes yet.

____

---

detachment [dɪ'tætʃmənt] Distanziertheit **to impair** [ɪm'peə] beeinträchtigen **undertaking** [ˌʌndə'teɪkɪŋ] Unternehmung

3. Does the future overrule the past?

____

4. We injected some mice with poison.

____

5. They caught Guy Fawkes.

____

6. They will train you in emotional detachment.

____

7. Lord Monteagle uncovered the plot.

____

8. They punished the Catholics.

____

9. This could impair your judgement.

____

10. You must study the entire process.

____

Johnson looked at Fanshawe, then turned and looked at Smith. Adrenalin was pumping through his veins and blood was racing to his head. His instincts told him to say yes immediately, but he was no fool; he knew that the dangers were real. "If things don't go according to plan, I mean, if something unexpected were to happen, is there some mechanism by which we would be able to return early?"

Smith looked as if she were desperately trying to force a comforting smile. "I'm afraid not, Professor. At least, not

yet. For the moment we have to set precise dates for departure and return. In your case, we would send you back to May 20th, 1604, and bring you back on January 31st, 1606 – one year, eight months, and eleven days later."
"The thirty-first of January?"
"The second day of **executions**. Guy Fawkes will be the last of the men to die, just before 8.30 in the morning at the Old Palace Yard at Westminster. We see no reason to keep you there any longer after that point."
Johnson sat up and **cleared his throat**. "Is there something I need to sign?"
As Fanshawe clapped his approval and delight, Smith leaned forward with a broad smile of satisfaction and relief. "Thank you. Now, Professor, I must remind you about what we call the **Sacred** Rule. Your job is to record history as it has already happened. **By virtue of** your presence in the past, you will be in a position to change history. I cannot stress to you enough that this is strictly forbidden. You must do nothing that would change the outcome of history. Do you understand?"
"Yes, of course."
Smith stood up. "Excellent. Then let's begin your training."

Three

In a quiet corner at the back of the *Duck and Drake* Inn, Johnson and Fanshawe sat close together at the corner of a table, barely visible in the **dim** candlelight. Johnson was

---

execution [ˌeksɪ'kjuːʃn] Hinrichtung **to clear one's throat** [ˌklɪə wʌnz 'θrəʊt] sich räuspern **sacred** ['seɪkrɪd] heilig **by virtue of** [baɪ 'vɜːtʃuː əv] aufgrund (von) **dim** [dɪm] halbdunkel

relieved to see that they looked much like all the other men there, dressed as they were in **linen breeches**, knee-length stockings and hunting shirts covered by **cloaks** – one scarlet, the other black. It had taken him several weeks of training to get used to the **itchy** clothes as well as the long pointed beard and **wide-brimmed** hat, but now it was his presence itself rather than his appearance that was making him self-conscious. As he looked around at the **sawdust** on the floor and the dark wooden **beams** that supported the ceiling, he saw the innkeeper staring at them from behind the bar and felt a sudden **dart** of fear, as if their true identities had been discovered within minutes of their arrival. It took him a moment to realize that the innkeeper would have known his customers well and was most likely just curious, not having seen these two strangers in his tavern before. Johnson assumed that the *Duck and Drake* was frequented by **merchants** and **traders** who lived and worked along the banks of the River Thames, a few minutes' walk from the fashionable Strand district where the inn was located. He worried that the man was also wondering why he had not seen them come in; it was likely that he had stood behind the bar all day, perhaps only having left in the early morning to collect the day's bread and meat from the market.

When the men had removed their hats and cloaks, Johnson cautiously approached the innkeeper. He was nervous; this was the first time he was speaking to someone since they

---

linen ['lɪnɪn] leinen- **breeches** ['brɪtʃɪz] Kniehose **cloak** [kləʊk] Umhang **itchy** ['ɪtʃɪ] juckend **wide-brimmed** ['waɪdbrɪmd] breitkrempig **sawdust** ['sɔːdʌst] Sägemehl **beam** [biːm] Balken **dart** [dɑːt] *hier:* Stich **merchant** ['mɜːtʃənt] Kaufmann **trader** ['treɪdə] Händler

had arrived, and all his training couldn't prevent a sick feeling in the **pit of his stomach**. He made a fist with his left hand and rubbed his thumb against the silver ring on his forefinger that Smith had given him a few minutes earlier, just prior to their departure. "For stressful situations," she had told him with a sympathetic smile. "When you feel anxious, rub this and think of something pleasant – a friend, a loved one, a happy memory, a peaceful landscape, a proud moment, an achievement. Think of something important, something bigger than the situation you find yourself in. Let it become a symbol of what's most important to you, a reminder of your real life." Up to that point he still had no idea of what it would be like to talk to people in the past, get to know them or, for goodness sake, to like them. All their training in the department, all the learning, hadn't prepared him for the real thing – it had just been theory. "Well then," he murmured. "Truth is the daughter of Time, and Time will tell."

As he crossed the floor of the tavern, Johnson tried to concentrate on an image of his mother's face. He was now a lot older than she had been when she died and the few memories of her that had stayed with him had become blurred by the passage of time. Now when he tried to **conjure up** an image of her, all that came to his mind were the photographs that he kept on his **mantelpiece**, four moments frozen in time that together recorded less than one hundredth of a second of her entire life. The images had become so familiar to him that he couldn't imagine any of the scenes an instant

---

pit of the stomach [ˈpɪt əv ðə ˈstʌmək] Magengrube **to conjure up sth.** [ˌkʌndʒər ˈʌp] etw. heraufbeschwören **mantelpiece** [ˈmæntlpiːs] Kaminsims

before or an instant after the pictures had been taken. In recent years he had found it increasingly **unsettling** to look at the photographs. They showed a happy, beautiful woman young enough to be his daughter; her early death had been an **affront** to the natural order of things, like a parent outliving a child. Now, however, he was barely five metres from the bar counter and the image of his mother faded quickly from his mind; he needed to concentrate on this, his first encounter in the past. His heartbeat increased when the innkeeper looked directly at him without smiling. Johnson kept one hand in his pocket, continuing to rub the ring, as he leaned on the bar counter with his right forearm.

"Two **ales** please. And might I ask whether you have rooms available?"

"How long will you be needing them?"

"Perhaps a week or two, if possible. We're not sure how long we will stay in London before returning to the North."

The innkeeper put the two mugs of dark brown beer on the counter. "Two ales, and two rooms. You can take your bags upstairs yourselves, if you don't mind. It'll be busy in here in a minute – the traders are finishing up for the day, and this place'll be **packed to the rafters** before long." He handed Johnson two keys. "Last two rooms at the end of the corridor on the left."

Johnson thanked him and **bowed** his head. He had been worried for weeks that his accent and his **grasp** of seventeenth century dialect would raise suspicions as soon as he arrived. He now felt a surge of relief at the success of this

---

unsettling [ˌʌnˈsetlɪŋ] beunruhigend **affront** [əˈfrʌnt] Beleidigung **packed to the rafters** [ˈpækt tə ðə ˈræftəz] gerammelt voll **to bow** [baʊ] neigen **grasp** [grɑːsp] *hier:* Verständnis

first encounter. "By the way," he added, as he picked up the keys and the beers, "I seem to **have lost track of time** on our journey. What is the date today?"

"Twentieth of May, I believe," the innkeeper replied, adding with a friendly smile, "all day. My name is Blake, by the way." *Perfect.* While historians had argued for centuries over many of the details of the plot, Johnson could find no disagreement in the history books about exactly when and where the **core group** of plotters had first agreed on their plan to kill King James and overthrow his government. The infamous meeting was to happen on this day, in this tavern.

Johnson and Fanshawe **sipped** their beers slowly as the *Duck and Drake* began to fill up. **Cobblers**, **tailors**, shopkeepers and fishermen poured in from the street alongside lawyers, knights, lords and **clergymen**. Soon the noise was so loud that the two men had to shout to hear each other. This hardly mattered, however, as they barely spoke a word; they were **mesmerized** by the scene before them.

Exercise 5: Cobblers, coopers and clergymen!

Insert the following 10 words beginning with "c" into the appropriate places in the text.

(crucial, candle, coming, came, Catesby, chill, centre, collective, committed, cast)

---

to lose (lost, lost) track of time [luːz / lɒst / lɒst ˌtræk əv ˈtaɪm] das Zeitgefühl verlieren **core group** [ˈkɔː gruːp] Kerngruppe **to sip** [sɪp] nippen an **cobbler** [ˈkɒblə] Schuster **tailor** [ˈteɪlə] Schneider **clergyman** [ˈklɜːdʒɪmən] Geistlicher **to be mesmerized** [biː ˈmezməraɪzd] gebannt sein

Five hours after they arrived, Johnson felt a **1.** ____________ as the front door of the tavern was pushed open from the outside. He **nudged** Fanshawe and **2.** ____________ his eyes in the direction of the five men who **3.** ____________ in. They walked purposefully towards the back of the inn and sat at a long table opposite Johnson and Fanshawe. When Blake brought five beers to their table, the men acknowledged him with a **4.** ____________ nod, although none of them smiled; Johnson knew that their serious expressions **betrayed** the importance of their meeting. They huddled together over the table and began whispering quietly, their faces **5.** ____________ in and out of view as they leaned towards each other over the **6.** ____________ at the **7.** ____________ of the table and away again.

All his adult life Johnson had been **8.** ____________ to gaining a deeper understanding of this exact period of history. To see these men before him now **in the flesh** was almost too much for his senses to register. He was briefly overwhelmed by feelings of **nausea**, and was terrified by the possibility that he might faint or **vomit**, or both, bringing

---

to nudge [nʌdʒ] (an)stupsen **to betray** [bɪ'treɪ] verraten
in the flesh [ɪn ðə 'fleʃ] leibhaftig **nausea** ['nɔːzɪə] Übelkeit
to vomit ['vɒmɪt] (sich er)brechen

unwanted attention upon himself at a **9.** ____________ moment. He had to sit up and take deep breaths, steadying his nerves by holding onto the table.

"This is it, Fanshawe, this is it! It's them! It's really them!"

"All right, Johnson, calm down, you're not at the Oscars. Any idea who's who?"

"The one sitting directly across from us at the head of the table, that's Robert **10.** ____________, the leader of the group and the brains behind the whole operation.

That's Guy Fawkes on his left. *Guy Fawkes, Fanshawe!* In the flesh! This is incredible. The two **chaps** opposite him are Thomas Percy and his brother-in-law Jack Wright, so the one with his back to us must be Tom Wintour. *Unbelievable*, Fanshawe."

The conversation between the five men was extremely difficult to hear, but early on Johnson clearly heard Percy speaking for a brief moment.

"Shall we always talk, gentlemen, and never do anything?"

The others quickly told him to keep his voice down. The plotters were obviously aware of how dangerous their discussion was, and now made sure that their whispers went no further than their own table. From time to time they glanced around to see if anyone was watching, forcing Johnson and Fanshawe to look away quickly. Catesby appeared to do most of the talking, while the others nodded

---

chap [tʃæp] Bursche

in agreement and rarely spoke. Only Fawkes remained completely silent throughout. After more than an hour had passed, Catesby stretched out his arm and slowly placed the palm of his hand flat on the table. One by one, his four co-conspirators laid their right hands on top of Catesby's. Johnson, who had been frustrated at his inability to hear the details of the discussion, now became excited again.

"This must be their **oath**. When the plot was uncovered, Fawkes and Wintour confessed that they had sworn an oath of loyalty and secrecy here at the *Duck and Drake*. They said that it was at this meeting that they had agreed to be blood brothers, loyal to each other and committed to killing King James and **overthrowing** his brutal anti-Catholic government."

The five men suddenly stood up from the table and quietly walked to the back door of the inn. Johnson and Fanshawe waited for a brief moment and then followed them out into the alleyway. To their right they saw a small, one-roomed wooden building with a flat roof just next to the *Duck and Drake*. They stood on either side of the door and pressed their ears against it. Johnson's heart was racing. They were no more than three or four metres away from the men; if the door opened now, they would be caught, questioned, and most likely killed.

After a few moments Johnson heard a single, deep voice from the other side of the door: "In the name of the Father, the Son, and the Holy Spirit. Amen. Heavenly Father, have mercy on us and hear our prayer. We praise you for giving us Jesus as our Saviour. He blessed the children who came to Him, and welcomes those who come to Him now. We

---

oath [əʊθ] Schwur **to overthrow** [ˌəʊvəˈθrəʊ] stürzen

believe that by His dying, Christ destroyed death for ever. May He give us everlasting life. He humbled Himself for our sake. May we follow His example and share in His **resurrection**. This day, the Father of Light has enlightened the minds of his **disciples**. We ask you, Lord, to bless these men and protect them with your love. May they grow in courage and in strength in your presence and in the sight of all. We ask this blessing, Father, through Your beloved Son, our Lord Jesus Christ, and the Holy Virgin Mary."

Johnson and Fanshawe hurried back to their table at the *Duck and Drake*. A few moments later, the five men walked slowly through the door, accompanied by a priest, and sat at their table again. They appeared more relaxed now, and soon they began to talk openly, laughing and chatting like any normal group of men enjoying a few drinks at their local tavern.

By now the noise in the tavern had become almost **deafening**. The beer **was taking its toll** on most of the drinkers. One after another men moved to the front door and emptied their **bladders** onto the street; passers-by had to be careful. Some didn't make it as far as the front door. Wooden buckets stood against the walls for those who couldn't or wouldn't go outside. The **stench** was so overwhelming that Johnson thought he was going to be sick several times those first few hours. The stink from some of the people was almost as bad as that from the buckets; when someone moved from one place to another, they left behind a sweet-sour

---

resurrection [ˌrezəˈrekʃn] Auferstehung **disciple** [dɪˈsaɪpl] Jünger **deafening** [ˈdefnɪŋ] ohrenbetäubend **to take (took, taken) its toll on sb.** [ˌteɪk / tʊk / ˈteɪkən ɪts ˈtəʊl ɒn] seinen Tribut fordern von jmdm. **bladder** [ˈblædə] Blase **stench** [stentʃ] Gestank

smell, heavy with dried sweat and dead skin. It hung so thick in the air that Johnson thought he could almost reach out and touch it. He listened closely as Catesby and the other five men avoided all talk about their plot. They spoke about the weather, about business, about *Troilus and Cressida* – the new play by William Shakespeare that was being performed at the Globe Theatre across the river.

As they talked and drank more beer, Johnson focussed intently on the behaviour and mannerisms of each man. He had read everything he could about each of them over the previous six months and was eager to find out if the historians had described them accurately. Most of the plotters were in their mid-thirties and related to each other by blood or marriage. Despite being members of the **landed gentry** with close links to powerful people, they found themselves in the position of a persecuted minority. They could neither graduate from university nor **pursue** careers in government, as they would have been forced to betray their religion by swearing the **Oath of Supremacy**, an acceptance of the monarch as the **Supreme Governor of the Church of England**. They were thus the first generation to find themselves born into a privileged class but with no possibility of enjoying these privileges without publicly abandoning their faith. With few career prospects, many men turned their attention to perfecting the skills associated with the **leisure pursuits** preferred by the gentry and

---

landed gentry [ˌlændɪd ˈdʒentrɪ] Landadel **to pursue** [pəˈsjuː] *hier:* nachgehen **Oath of Supremacy** [ˌəʊθ əv sʊˈpreməsɪ] Suprematseid **Supreme Governor of the Church of England** [suːˈpriːm ˌɡʌvnə əv ðə ˌtʃɜːtʃ əv ˈɪŋɡlənd] Oberhaupt der Anglikanischen Kirche **leisure pursuit** [ˈleʒə pəˌsjuːt] Freizeitbeschäftigung

nobility – hunting, **horsemanship**, and **swordsmanship**. This combination of skills, coupled with anger and resentment at their persecution and limited career opportunities, led many men to leave England and fight in Europe, mainly on the side of Catholic Spain and the Spanish-controlled Netherlands in the ongoing hostilities with Protestant England. The small group of men now sitting opposite Johnson were a perfect example of such **disaffected** men. Not all had fought in Europe, however. Some had had little opportunity, as they had spent much of their adult life behind bars. Robert Catesby had been imprisoned in 1596 **merely** as a **precautionary measure** when Queen Elizabeth I was ill. In the Tower of London he was held alongside three men who would eventually become key members of the Gunpowder Plot. Catesby was clearly a confident, **gregarious** man – a natural leader and an impressive speaker. Known to his friends as Robin, he was admired for his keen intellect and magnetic charm. In every account that Johnson had managed to find, Catesby had been variously described as 'courageous and **dashing**', 'handsome and **courteous**', 'generous and **affable**'. He had supposedly converted more Protestants to Catholicism than any priest, and historians believed that without Catesby's mesmerizing personality the group of men who conspired to blow up King James would never have come together. He let his eyes drift over the

---

horsemanship ['hɔːsmənʃɪp] Reitkunst **swordsmanship** ['sɔːdmənʃɪp] Fechtkunst **disaffected** [ˌdɪsə'fektɪd] unzufrieden **merely** ['mɪəlɪ] bloß **precautionary measure** [prɪ'kɔːʃənərɪ ˌmeʒə] Vorsichtsmaßnahme **gregarious** [grɪ'geərɪəs] gesellig **dashing** ['dæʃɪŋ] elegant **courteous** ['kɜːtɪəs] höflich **affable** ['æfəbl] leutselig

table and recognized the other men as Thomas Percy, Tom Wintour, Jack Wright and Guy Fawkes, or, as he preferred to be known, Guido. Johnson didn't recognize the sixth man, but although he wore similar clothes to the others, Johnson knew that he must be the Jesuit priest Father John Gerard.

Exercise 6: Which word is the odd one out?
Circle the appropriate letter.

1. **a.** treason **b.** plot
   c. rebellion **d.** treasure
2. **a.** skill **b.** smell
   c. stench **d.** stink
3. **a.** dashing **b.** ugly
   c. handsome **d.** good-looking
4. **a.** cowardly **b.** gallant
   c. brave **d.** courageous
5. **a.** gregarious **b.** charming
   c. courteous **d.** unsociable
6. **a.** argumentative **b.** reflective
   c. quiet **d.** mild-mannered

The conversation stopped suddenly when the front door flew open and a young woman in a long, flowing blue dress came rushing in. Carrying a small child in her arms, she looked terribly **distressed** as she moved quickly towards the corner where the plotters sat. Johnson could see that the boy looked ill and immediately wondered if he had contracted the **plague**. Thousands were still dying from it all across London and no one knew how to prevent or cure

---

distressed [dɪ'strest] bekümmert **plague** [pleɪg] Pest

it. Catesby jumped up, looking highly surprised to see this woman running towards the men, who cleared their mugs off the table and moved the candle to the edge.

"Catherine? What are you doing here? Is Robert all right?"

"Robin, do something – I think he's dying!" As the men helped to lay the boy out on the table, his mother fell to her knees and **wept** uncontrollably. Although her long black hair covered her face and her hands were pressed against her pale cheeks, her cries could be heard throughout the tavern. The other customers lowered their voices and looked on with **uneasy** pity, but none rose to offer help or support.

Johnson watched Robin, who was looking helplessly at his son; the child's skin was pale and he was exhausted from trying to vomit. The priest began to pray quietly over his body, hoping that nobody would notice and identify him as a **man of the cloth**.

"He's dying, Robin. Oh, dear God, please don't do this to me again, I beg of you."

Johnson knew that Catherine's and Robin's first son, William, had died in the mid-1590s at a young age and remembered having seen a reference to Catesby's second son having lived a long life. Knowing that Robert was going to survive, he knew immediately that it was safe to take a risk and make a connection with the plotters. He stood up quickly and walked over to Catherine. "Excuse me, Madam, please forgive my **intrusion**, but I'm a doctor and I couldn't help but notice that your son is ill. Might I ask if he has had **diarrhoea**?"

---

to weep (wept, wept) [wiːp / wept / wept] weinen **uneasy** [ʌnˈiːzɪ] unbehaglich **man of the cloth** [ˌmæn əv ðə ˈklɒθ] Geistlicher **intrusion** [ɪnˈtruːʒn] Störung **diarrhoea** [ˌdaɪəˈrɪə] Durchfall

Catherine wiped the tears from her dark eyes with the back of her hand, still **sniffling** and shaking as she looked up. "Yes, since last night. And vomiting."
Johnson turned to the innkeeper who was staring at the scene from behind the bar.
"It is."
"Good. I will need you to boil some water and leave it boiling for ten minutes. Can you please do this? And bring me a cold, damp cloth." Johnson prayed that the child was simply dehydrated. He knew that some clean water mixed with the right amount of salt and sugar would rehydrate the boy, and regardless of what illness he had this simple treatment would be of some benefit.
When Blake returned, Johnson gently cleaned the boy's face with the damp cloth and dabbed his forehead. Catesby looked at Johnson with an expression of respect. "I must thank you sincerely, sir, for your **generosity** and quick action. You must be a most **accomplished** doctor. May I ask your name?"
"Anthony Johnson, and this is my friend and colleague Dr Peter Fanshawe." Fanshawe smiled and bowed his head. "It is a pleasure to meet you, Mr … ?"
"Catesby, Robin Catesby. This is my wife Catherine. This is Mr Thomas Percy, Mr Thomas Wintour, Mr John Wright, Mr Guy Fawkes, and Father John Gerard." Catesby suddenly **winced** as if he were in pain. Johnson could see that he had recognized his error as soon as he had said it; calling Gerard 'Father' was a careless and dangerous **blunder** that,

---

to sniffle ['snɪfl] schniefen **generosity** [ˌdʒenə'rɒsətɪ] Großzügigkeit **accomplished** [ə'kʌmplɪʃt] begabt **to wince** [wɪns] zusammenzucken **blunder** ['blʌndə] grober Fehler

under different circumstances, could have cost the priest his life. Johnson leaned towards him and quietly said, "It's all right, my friend, we too are Catholics."
"Thank God," said Catesby, visibly relieved. "These are dangerous times for us, Dr Johnson."
"Dangerous times indeed," Johnson replied in a low voice. "If only there were something that could be done about the situation before this foolish king has us all in chains. How long does he think he can continue to persecute us? A year? A decade? A century?"
Blake arrived back with the pot of boiling water. Johnson thanked him and asked if he would also bring some salt and sugar. The innkeeper went back to the kitchen and brought out two small bowls. Johnson waited for the water to cool down before adding some salt and sugar, stirring it **vigorously** for almost a minute. He gently lifted the boy's head and whispered to him, "Come now, drink this, it will help to make you feel better."
Robert coughed and **spluttered** as he tried to drink; much of the mixture spilled down his chin and across his cheeks, but he managed to take in about half of it. Johnson bent down and spoke gently to Catherine who sat **impassively** at the table, looking physically exhausted and emotionally **drained**. "You must take this child home and repeat this procedure. Give him as much of this mixture as he will take. Do you understand?"
Catherine pushed the hair back from her face and nodded. "Will he live? Please, just tell me that he will live."
"Don't worry, Mrs Catesby, your son will be well as long as

---

vigorously ['vigərəslɪ] energisch **to splutter** ['splʌtə] prusten
impassively [ɪm'pæsɪvlɪ] teilnahmslos **drained** [dreɪnd] ausgelaugt

you keep him cool and continue to give him this treatment."

"Thank you so much, Dr Johnson. May God bless you."

Catherine didn't have the energy to say anything more; she took her son in her arms and left the *Duck and Drake* without a word or a glance towards her husband or the others. Johnson wondered how Catesby could watch her leave and remain in the tavern with his friends. Was he a cold man? Was there no warmth between Catesby and his wife? Did he not care for his own son? Was it expected in the seventeenth century that a child's problems would **solely** be the concern of the mother? Or **had** the plot **consumed** Catesby to the point that it was more important than his own family? Johnson reminded himself that he was not to judge the values or behaviour of the people he met, and forced an awkward smile in Catesby's direction.

As soon as Catherine left, Catesby invited Johnson and Fanshawe to join the men at their table. As they all sat down, Guy Fawkes looked at the professor and shook his head in **admiration**. "That was most impressive, Dr Johnson. Why have we never heard of such a treatment before?"

Johnson cleared his throat, trying hard to act normally, and searching desperately for an explanation that would sound **authoritative** and believable. He had never had trouble speaking to an auditorium full of students, had enjoyed it, in fact, but now he felt utterly lost and helpless. Fanshawe saved him the trouble. "It's a very new discovery, Mr Fawkes. Only in the past few months have we tested it with

---

solely ['səʊllɪ] auschließlich **to consume sb.** [kən'sjuːm] jmdn. in Anspruch nehmen **admiration** [ˌædmə'reɪʃn] Bewunderung **authoritative** [ɔː'θɒrətətɪv] maßgebend

success, and we still don't know how or why it works, but it does."

All his life Johnson had found it difficult to lie. As a child, his grandmother had told him she could tell if he was lying by reading his thoughts. She would stand at his side and gently tug his ear, pretending to look deep into his mind. The little boy was terrified, desperately trying to force out any impure thoughts that he didn't want her to see. He was quietly impressed to see that Fanshawe didn't seem to suffer from the same **anxieties**.

"In fact," Fanshawe continued, seeming to gain confidence with every word, "Dr Johnson is being most modest. It was he who discovered the treatment. Why don't you tell our new friends how you came upon it?"

"Is that so?" asked Percy, who now sat up and stared at Johnson. "Tell us, Doctor, how did you come to develop such an important **remedy**?"

Johnson couldn't believe what Fanshawe was doing. Had he lost his mind? Was he trying to get them killed? Johnson needed to get the conversation back to King James; he wanted to **plant the seed in** Catesby's **mind** that he and Fanshawe might be valuable allies, perhaps even co-conspirators.

"Well," he began, still trying to think of something to say as he **averted** his eyes from the **gaze** of the men, "It was an accident. A close friend of mine in the North, a priest by the name of Father Edward Browne, had been imprisoned. He had been badly beaten and was suffering terribly. After

---

anxiety [æŋ'zaɪətɪ] Sorge **remedy** ['remədɪ] Heilmittel **to plant a seed in sb.'s mind** [ˌplɑːnt ə 'siːd ɪn / 'maɪnd] jmdm. etw. suggerieren **to avert** [ə'vɜːt] abwenden **gaze** [geɪz] Blick

three months, he managed to escape from his captors. Not knowing where to go, he arrived at my house in a terrible state of weakness and disease. His symptoms were much the same as those of your son, Mr Catesby, and he said he was very thirsty. Before he arrived I had been boiling water to make some soup. I was reaching up to get a spoon when one of my shelves came loose, and I knocked some salt and sugar into the water. I had no more water and so I gave what I had to Father Browne. He drank the whole pot during the night and by the next morning he was beginning to show signs of improvement."

Exercise 7: Underline the correct part of speech – adjective or adverb?

1. Catherine was *(desperate/desperately)* afraid that her son would die.
2. Johnson thought *(hard/hardly)* and then came up with an idea.
3. The little boy was feeling *(bad/badly)*.
4. He was suffering from a *(rapid/rapidly)* loss of fluids.
5. Johnson gave the mixture a *(vigorous/vigorously)* stir.
6. Catesby showed *(visible/visibly)* signs of relief.
7. Catherine should keep her son *(cool/coolly)*.
8. Johnson explained everything away *(convincing/convincingly)* and *(good/well)*.

Johnson thought this was the most **ridiculous** story, but he knew that Catesby had harboured a priest who had escaped from prison some years earlier, and hoped that the story would come across as evidence of his sympathy with their

---

ridiculous [rɪˈdɪkjʊləs] lächerlich

cause, rather than as a highly suspicious coincidence. His gamble paid off; Catesby looked at him with an expression of great respect. "You are a most courageous man, Dr Johnson, most courageous."
"It's kind of you to say so, but I did nothing special. I gave some food, water, and shelter to a poor soul in desperate need. In times such as these, we cannot turn our backs on each other. What crime had Father Browne committed that he deserved such treatment? Why should we be treated as criminals and slaves simply because we **maintain** the religious traditions that have served this country well for more than a thousand years? Why should we be **despised** as 'God's **lunatics**'? Why should we have to live in fear? This country has become a sick place. The whole nation has been **afflicted by** a deadly disease."
Catesby looked at the other men and after a long silence turned to Johnson and Fanshawe. "Gentlemen, the disease of which you speak calls for a powerful remedy, and I believe that with your help we will be in a position to **administer** it. If you are interested, meet Guido and myself tomorrow morning after breakfast on the steps of St Paul's Cathedral. I assure you that you will not be disappointed."

Four

Fanshawe was surprised to see Guido and Robin already waiting on the steps of St Paul's Cathedral, as he and John-

---

to maintain [meɪn'teɪn] bewahren **to be despised** [bi: dɪ'spaɪzd] verachtet werden **lunatic** ['lu:nətɪk] Wahnsinniger **to be afflicted by sth.** [bi: ə'flɪktɪd baɪ] unter etw. leiden **to administer** [əd'mɪnɪstə] verabreichen

son had arrived half an hour earlier than the agreed time. They greeted each other quickly and began to walk west along the bend in the river that led to Westminster. Although Fanshawe clearly remembered how often they had been told during training not to stare at people and places when they arrived, he found it almost impossible to concentrate on what Catesby was saying; he was too busy looking around him, his mouth open in astonishment at the sights and smells before him. Instead of the **hydrogen-powered** cars and **magnetic levitation** trams that he was used to seeing on the streets of his native city, he now saw more animals than people; horses and **donkeys** trotted up and down the wide dirt tracks, pigs and chickens hunted in piles of rubbish for **edible scraps**, ducks and geese wandered about unsupervised. Traders battled through the streets, carrying their merchandise on **rickety** wooden carts, calling out their list of wares for sale in a deafening cacophony. Women in shawls threw buckets of **filthy** water from doors and windows onto the streets below while shouting at children who ran and played in the dirt outside. Once the crowds had thinned out a little, Catesby stopped suddenly and turned to Fanshawe and Johnson. "We're taking you to a place near the Parliament where we can discuss in detail the issues that we spoke about last night."

Fanshawe stopped looking around and did his best to focus on what Catesby was saying but he couldn't help feeling

---

hydrogen-powered [ˈhaɪdrədʒənˌpaʊəd] wasserstoffbetrieben
magnetic levitation [mægˌnetɪk ˌlevɪˈteɪʃn] Magnetschwebe-
donkey [ˈdɒŋkɪ] Esel **edible** [ˈedəbl] essbar **scrap** [skræp] Rest
rickety [ˈrɪkətɪ] klapprig **filthy** [ˈfɪlθɪ] dreckig

slightly amused by the earnest expression on Catesby's face. There was something about the **inevitability** of how the plot would **unravel** that prevented Fanshawe from taking it too seriously. Although he was now here in the past, staring directly at two key figures in British history, he felt **disconnected** from his surroundings. His frame of mind was that of a **theatre-goer**, of someone who had made a conscious decision to engage emotionally with the cast of characters, but solely for the purposes of entertainment and **distraction**.

Catesby lowered his voice and leaned closer to the other men. "We all agree that something must be done about our monarch and his **treacherous** government, do we not?"

Fanshawe nodded his agreement with as much **solemnity** as he could **muster** while Catesby continued. "We are taking a great risk in telling you this, but we pray that you will join us. Many of us have suffered for our religion. I myself was imprisoned, having committed no greater crime than accommodating a Jesuit priest. My father before me was also imprisoned. Our status as members of the gentry did not protect us. This situation, my friends, is going to end." Catesby paused for a moment to ensure he had their full attention. "We are going to **assassinate** King James."

Fanshawe drew a deep breath and put his hand to his mouth, doing his best to look surprised. "Robin, no!" De-

---

inevitability [ɪnˌevɪtəˈbɪlətɪ] Unvermeidbarkeit **to unravel** [ʌnˈrævl] zunichte gemacht werden **disconnected** [ˌdɪskəˈnektɪd] losgelöst **theatre-goer** [ˈθɪətəˌɡəʊə] Theaterbesucher **distraction** [dɪˈstrækʃn] Ablenkung **treacherous** [ˈtretʃərəs] verräterisch **solemnity** [səˈlemnətɪ] Ernst **to muster** [ˈmʌstə] aufbringen **to assassinate** [əˈsæsɪneɪt] ermorden

spite his intensive training, however, his sense of distance from the events had obviously affected his acting skills; Fanshawe could see by the expression on Fawkes's face that he hadn't been convincing enough.

"Dr Fanshawe, do you think we are not serious?"

Fanshawe quickly wiped the smile off his face. "Forgive me, Mr Fawkes, but are you trying to tell us that you plan to *murder* King James? That's absurd!"

"First of all, Dr Fanshawe, it will not be murder. The King, by his actions, **has forfeited** his right to govern and it is our duty to replace him."

Fanshawe was wondering how to respond convincingly when Johnson intervened. "Gentlemen, I'm sure Dr Fanshawe is expressing disbelief rather than disapproval. After all, this is rather dramatic news. How can you possibly expect to succeed? Surely the country will be in a more dangerous state if the King is killed than it is now?"

"We plan not only to kill the King, Dr Johnson, but to eliminate most of his government at the same time. We will capture the King's young daughter, Elizabeth, and install her as Queen. She will be raised a Catholic, and we will make sure that she marries a Catholic. However, we know that our actions will have a **widespread impact** around the country. We are going to raise a rebellion in the Midlands and the North with the help of Catholic exiles now fighting under the Spanish flag in Europe. But before we go any further, I need to know if you are with us. If you doubt our ability to succeed, I can only tell you that our plans are

---

to forfeit ['fɔ:fɪt] verwirken **widespread** ['waɪdspred] weit verbreitet **impact** ['ɪmpækt] Auswirkung

already at an advanced stage. If you agree to join us now in principle, we will provide more details which I believe will persuade you that we *will* succeed."

Fanshawe looked at Johnson briefly, pretending to be overwhelmed by what he had just heard. He moved closer to the men, putting a hand on each of the conspirator's shoulders. "Robin, Guido, you have my full support. I'm with you in this. Anthony?"

Johnson **furrowed his brow** and stared into the distance as if he were thinking through the implications of joining the plotters. Eventually he began to nod his head slowly. "Yes. This situation has to be ended. **Count me in.**"

A wide smile broke across Catesby's face. He slapped the men's backs in delight and urged them to move on. "Wonderful. The two of you will be **invaluable** to our efforts, absolutely invaluable."

They walked with a purpose now, getting closer and closer to Parliament. When they finally reached Westminster, Fanshawe was **taken aback**. Without Big Ben hanging in its famous tower, which would not be built for another two hundred and fifty-four years, the old Parliament seemed less powerful, less imposing, less threatening. Comparing in his mind the Houses of Parliament from his time with the buildings before him, he realized that a lot would change over the centuries. Johnson had of course done his research: he knew that a good part of the Houses of Parliament was built in the nineteenth century.

---

to furrow one's brow [ˌfʌrəʊ wʌnz ˈbraʊ] die Stirn runzeln **Count me in.** [ˌkaʊnt mɪ ˈɪn] Ihr könnt auf mich zählen. **invaluable** [ɪnˈvæljʊəbl] unschätzbar **to be taken aback** [biː ˌteɪkən əˈbæk] verblüfft sein

Exercise 8: Some of the following advice taken from an old guidebook to London is anachronistic. Which four tips would not make sense in early seventeenth-century London?

1. Enjoy the sound of Big Ben striking the hour.
2. Watch out for geese roaming the streets.
3. Be careful of the rickety carts.
4. Ask your landlord where you can attend Catholic Mass.
5. Don't worry! You can drink the water.
6. Taverns can be somewhat smelly.
7. Buckets are provided in taverns for you to take ale home with you.
8. St Paul's Cathedral is worth a visit.

Finally they entered a house through the back and went quickly to a door behind the stairs that led down to the basement. As they descended the steps to an underground room, Fanshawe thought he could hear the sound of metal on rock. There was somebody down there – perhaps more than one person.

The noise stopped abruptly as a chilly, damp room came into view, lit by dozens of small candles. Catesby finally broke the silence. "Gentlemen, you remember Mr Percy, Mr Wright, and Mr Wintour from last evening, don't you?"

The three men stepped forward into the light and greeted Fanshawe and Johnson warmly. Although the empty room was cold, **beads of sweat** were dripping from their foreheads and the tips of their noses. They put down the large **pickaxes** they were holding and raised their dirty shirt sleeves to wipe the sweat from their faces. Catesby began to

---

bead of sweat [ˌbiːd əv ˈswet] Schweißperle **pickaxe** [ˈpɪkæks] Hacke

explain what was going on. "This wall, gentlemen, is precisely one hundred and thirty-three feet from the **foundation wall** of His Majesty's Parliament. With your help, we are going to **dig** a tunnel from this room to a point beneath the House of Lords. When we reach that point, we will plant enough gunpowder to blow James and his government into a million bloody pieces. The tunnel will take a long, long time to dig – we know that – but patience is the key to the success of our mission."
None of the men, including Fanshawe and Johnson, were used to manual labour. Catesby and the others were aristocratic gentlemen who had servants to do any physical labour they required. Fanshawe sighed. The tunnel was going to take a very long time indeed.

By the time they arrived back at the *Duck and Drake* in the early evening, Fanshawe was exhausted. His muscles ached as if he had just spent the day running a marathon or working in the fields. As they sat down to a plate of dirty fish and **lumpy** brown ale, served up to them by a smiling Blake, Fanshawe realized that his usual cheerful **demeanour was** slowly **abandoning** him; seventeenth-century life was already taking its toll. "Christ, what I wouldn't do right now for a hot shower and some clean clothes."
Johnson looked at him, raising an eyebrow as if Fanshawe were a student who had said something foolish in one of his classes. "Peter, how many times did we talk about this in training?"

---

foundation wall ['faʊndeɪʃn wɔːl] Grundmauer **to dig (dug, dug)** [dɪg / dʌg / dʌg] graben **lumpy** ['lʌmpɪ] klumpig **demeanour** [dɪ'miːnə] *hier:* Gemüt **to abandon** [ə'bændən] verlassen

Fanshawe stopped rubbing his thighs and turned to Johnson, giving him a look of hurt and disbelief at his lack of empathy. “Thanks, Anthony, there’s nothing like a little mutual support and encouragement to keep the team spirit alive.”

“You’ll just get frustrated if you think about things you can’t have.”

Fanshawe didn’t appear to be listening to him. “I think I’m getting a **rash** on the inside of my thighs.”

Johnson looked sadly at the piece of fish clinging to his fork before slowly returning it to his plate. “Nice, Fanshawe. Thanks for that.”

“Don’t mention it. By the way, while we were digging the tunnel today, I started to think about something that’s been bothering me. It’s not just that we both know about the tunnel. Now that we’re part of the group, surely the men who are caught when the plot fails will mention us when they’re tortured?”

“I expect they will, yes.”

“So why aren’t our names already in the history books? I’ve tried to think of a scientific explanation but I can’t figure it out. I mean, to the best of my knowledge we are actually here, and not in some parallel universe alongside the universe of these people. I can see no scientific reason why our names shouldn’t be recorded.”

“I think it might actually be quite **straightforward**. Some of the men were tortured for days after being caught, and there’s obviously no **verbatim record** of those sessions, so we can only speculate about what happened, can’t we?”

---

rash [ræʃ] Ausschlag **straightforward** [ˌstreɪtˈfɔːwəd] unkompliziert **verbatim record** [vɜːˈbeɪtɪm ˌrekɔːd] wörtliches Protokoll

"Obviously."
"It stands to reason, though, that the men would have lied for as long as possible in order to protect the others and their families. The King's torturers would therefore have had to listen to stories that were partly true and partly false. When the pain became too intense and the men started telling the truth, the **interrogators** would still be suspicious about what was true and what wasn't."
"Go on."
"Ten of the men were related through blood or marriage, and almost all of them had already had some kind of previous **run-in** with the law. They were well-known to the authorities and it wouldn't have taken long to draw up the list. In fact, the only member who wasn't known to the government was Guy Fawkes himself, and he was the first to be caught. You also have to remember that five of the core group – the men who knew most about the plot – were shot dead before they could be interrogated."
"So you're saying they simply didn't believe the men when they mentioned us?"
"I'm saying they would have looked into it and discovered that there were no such people as Anthony Johnson and Peter Fanshawe. There were no doctors from the north of England with those names. The interrogators would have assumed that the story about you and me was part of the lies told by the men under torture, especially if they had named us towards the beginning of the torture. It would have been assumed that they made up these names in order to protect their real friends and families. If they couldn't

---

interrogator [ɪnˈterəgeɪtə] Vernehmungsbeamter **run-in** [rʌnˈɪn] Zusammenstoß

find any evidence that you and I existed, and they knew that they had no chance of capturing us, they would also want to keep it quiet that there might **be** two plotters still **on the loose**. They would have wanted to assure the public that all the plotters were dead or **in custody**. It was in their interest not to have our names mentioned outside the torture cells."

"So there would be no official record about us."

"Precisely. On the other hand, you have the **extended families** of the men and many other people who helped to hide Jesuit priests and were sympathetic to the Catholic cause, but probably knew nothing about the plot itself. The government had no problem pointing the finger at this group and punishing them severely for their very **tenuous** connection to the plot."

Fanshawe nodded slowly, turning back to his meal. When they finished eating, the two men sat in silence for several minutes as they watched the comings and goings in the tavern with child-like fascination for a second night. As Fanshawe stared at the crowd, his thoughts turned to the men with whom he had spent the day. Before he arrived, his mind had been occupied with the technical challenges of the **assignment**, and with Johnson taking the lead on the historical aspects Fanshawe had had little reason to devote much thought to the plotters themselves. Indeed, he had found it almost impossible to imagine them as real people; but now, having met them and spent the day digging the

---

to be on the loose [biː ɒn ðə ˈluːs] frei herumlaufen **in custody** [ɪn ˈkʌstədɪ] in Haft **extended family** [ɪkˌstendɪd ˈfæmlɪ] Großfamilie **tenuous** [ˈtenjʊəs] schwach **assignment** [əˈsaɪnmənt] Auftrag

tunnel with them, he thought about their **determination**, their courage, their sense of solidarity, the risks they were willing to take and the horrors they were prepared to inflict in order to bring about a more just and tolerant regime. He turned and looked Johnson in the eye.

"Imagine if they had succeeded."

"What?"

"Catesby and the others. Imagine if they had actually managed to kill the king and overthrow the government."

"Oh Fanshawe, don't start that, *please*."

"Why not? Just because Smith thinks it's dangerous for us to ..."

"She's right. It *is* dangerous. We have enough to do without confusing matters by speculating on what might have happened. What happened happened. We're not going to change it. We're going to record it. All right?"

"How can you be so insensitive? Can't you even allow yourself to imagine what it must be like for these men? Look at the risks they're taking. Look at the lengths they're willing to go to. They really believe in what they're doing."

"Well, of course they believe in what they're doing, Fanshawe. I don't think that was ever doubted."

"Yes, but maybe they believe in it so strongly because it's the right thing to do. Maybe it really is. Christ, Johnson, we have been close to these people, we have spoken to them, we are getting to know them, really know them, we are beginning to like them. These are real people! How can we not get involved? We know what their dreams are, and we share ..."

But Johnson interrupted him, shaking his head. "Fanshawe, we're here to do a job, not to agree or disagree with

---

determination [dɪˌtɜːmɪˈneɪʃn] Entschlossenheit

the morality or **justification** of what they're doing, and certainly not to **interfere**. For God's sake, you've been with the Department since the beginning. It's your rule!"
Fanshawe's blood was boiling at Johnson's **condescending** tone. Who the hell did he think he was? He had no right to give orders to anyone. "It was never my rule. It was a political decision, taken without consulting me. As far as they're concerned, I'm just the technician."
"Whatever. Just don't get any ideas about **meddling**." For Johnson, this seemed to be the last word on the matter.
Fanshawe knew it was pointless to continue the conversation. He shot Johnson a look of extreme irritation, finished his drink quickly, and went up to his room.

They returned to the house the next morning to continue digging the tunnel. Percy arrived a little later than the rest, carrying a heavy sack over his shoulder. He opened it and turned it upside down, spilling out hundreds of candles to keep the room lit as the work progressed. Fanshawe was impressed by how well the men got on, keeping each other's spirits up with stories and jokes throughout the long days of hard work. He admired their **resilience** and their strength; none of them ever complained about their aches and pains.

After a month or so, they had made enough progress to feel that they were finally getting somewhere. They brought in heavy wooden beams and fixed them to the walls of the

---

justification [ˌdʒʌstɪfɪˈkeɪʃn] Rechtfertigung **to interfere** [ˌɪntəˈfɪə] eingreifen **condescending** [ˌkɒndɪˈsendɪŋ] herablassend **to meddle** [ˈmedl] sich einmischen **resilience** [rɪˈzɪlɪəns] Standhaftigkeit

tunnel for support; none of them was an expert in construction, and they didn't want to risk having the roof collapse on top of them. For Fanshawe, however, the constant swinging of the pickaxe felt too much like hard work. Johnson had told him that he also felt **dispirited** at times, not so much because of the backbreaking labour, but because he knew that the tunnel was not going to work. As the hours turned into days and the days into weeks, he tried to stop himself from thinking about the **inevitable** failure of the tunnel and to concentrate on the work at hand, focussing on the challenge of **chipping at** the rock, one tiny piece at a time.

Exercise 9: Put the verbs into either the Past Simple or the Past Continuous.

1. They *(realize)* ____________________ that three figures *(stand)* ____________________ in the shadows.
2. They put down the axes they *(hold)* ____________________ when the strangers *(arrive)* ____________________.
3. Fanshaw *(yawn)* ____________________ when he *(enter)* ____________________ the *Duck and Drake.*
4. When they *(spot)* ____________________ Blake, he *(smile)* ____________________.
5. Fanshawe *(realize)* ____________________ that seventeenth century life *(take)* ____________________ its toll.

---

dispirited [dɪ'spɪrɪtɪd] niedergeschlagen **inevitable** [ɪn'evɪtəbl] unvermeidlich **to chip at sth.** ['tʃɪp ət] etw. abtragen

6. Something *(occur)* ____________________ to Fanshawe when they *(dig)* ____________________ the tunnel.

7. Percy *(carry)* ____________________ a heavy sack over his shoulder when he *(arrive)* ____________________.

8. Fanshawe *(sit)* ____________________ on the stairs when he *(hear)* ____________________ a loud, confident voice.

On a terribly hot day in late June, after they had finished working for the day, all seven went to the *Duck and Drake* to discuss their progress. After a good talk and several beers, Catesby stretched his hands across the table towards Fanshawe and Johnson. "My friends, you have both been invaluable to our efforts and I feel that we are now blood brothers, but I worry for your safety as much as for that of the other men. This inn is no place for men such as you to stay. You deserve a home to stay in while you are in London and a refuge from the dangers of James's network of **spies**. They spend almost all their time in places like this. Tomorrow you will leave this tavern and bring your things to my house. From now on you will be my guests."
Johnson tried to object but Catesby closed his eyes and shook his head. "I won't hear another word about it. I would only say to you that our oath of secrecy extends also to my home, and we cannot discuss the plot there. Good; then my servant, Bates, will be here at ten o'clock to bring you to my house. We will have your rooms prepared by then. I think you will find it a little more comfortable – and perhaps a great deal safer – than the *Duck and Drake*."

---

spy [spaɪ] Spion

Five

Johnson was relieved to be leaving his **dingy** room above the *Duck and Drake*. He had become used to the dirt and the smell, but the noise was **intolerable** and it was impossible to get a good night's sleep in his sticky, **humid** room. What he had been given to sleep on was bed-shaped, but that was the extent of the similarity to his own temperature-controlled **quilt** and mattress back in the twenty-first century. His muscles ached permanently from the digging during the day and poor sleep at night. At the same time, however, he felt that he might miss the place a little; it had been the place where they arrived, and their home for nearly two months. He had become quite fond of Blake, and enjoyed watching the crowds in the evenings.

Fanshawe told him he was being unnecessarily sentimental. "It's a **hovel**, Johnson, and we're finally getting out. Don't get sentimental on me about this rat-infested hole. Please."

Catesby's servant, Thomas Bates, was waiting for them when they came down to pay Blake and say their goodbyes. He took their bags and brought them to the northern outskirts of the city. It didn't take very long; London was by far the largest city in Europe in 1604, but tiny in comparison with the London they were familiar with. They arrived at a large, **two-storey** mansion, standing in its own private grounds, surrounded by tall **oak trees**.

---

dingy ['dɪndʒɪ] schäbig **intolerable** [ɪn'tɒlərəbl] unerträglich **humid** ['hju:mɪd] feucht **quilt** [kwɪlt] Steppdecke **hovel** ['hɒvl] Bruchbude **two-storey** ['tu:stɔ:rɪd] zweistöckig **oak (tree)** ['əʊk tri:] Eiche

As they walked towards the house, Catesby appeared at the front door and descended the steps to greet them.
Once they were inside and sitting in the living room, Catherine arrived with hot drinks and snacks. Johnson hadn't seen Catesby's wife since the night she came rushing into the *Duck and Drake* carrying her sick child in her arms. He hadn't realized that night how beautiful she was; the excitement of their arrival in the past, the risk of pretending they were medical doctors, the noise and smell of the inn, and the urgency of young Robert's illness had left little time to step back and notice her long black hair and the way it fell across the pale, perfect skin of her face. He hadn't had a chance to notice the **dimples** that appeared in her cheeks when she smiled shyly, lowering her eyes and tilting her head to one side as she did so. Johnson felt a dart of pain in his chest when he realized just how closely Catherine resembled the woman he had nearly married four hundred and forty years later. In the end he had pushed Ruth away from him. His therapist told him that he was afraid of commitment, but Johnson knew that this was not the reason. He was extremely committed and loyal to his friends, so much so that he lived in fear of losing the love of those close to him. His mother had died tragically when he was a young boy and he **had vowed** never again to love someone so much in case they were taken away from him; he knew that he would not be able to cope with such a loss twice in his life.
When he met Ruth, however, he had realized the foolishness of his childhood vow; love was not something that could be so easily decided upon. Logic, reason, rationality

---

dimple ['dɪmpl] Grübchen **to vow** [vaʊ] geloben

and self-protection were worthless defences against the overpowering force of love. They did little more than create feelings of **vulnerability** and anxiety in Johnson; his fear of losing Ruth made his behaviour erratic and intense. The relationship eventually became too claustrophobic for her; she felt that Johnson **was monitoring** her all the time, judging her actions and questioning her friendships. When she could stand it no longer, she packed her things and left.

Johnson's heart skipped a beat when Catherine greeted him first. As she moved quickly towards him, he found himself staring down at the cap in his hand. "Doctor, what a pleasure. I wondered when we would meet again. And it is such an honour to have you in our home. I can't thank you enough for what you did for Robert – you saved his life. I wish we had met you when our first son was ill. Unfortunately he wasn't as lucky as Robert." Just then, the child came crawling through from the next room as quickly as his little hands and knees could carry him, making straight for his mother with the determination of a wild animal in search of food.

Johnson focussed all his attention on him in order to avoid eye contact with Catherine. He felt sure that the others would easily read his thoughts from the look in his eyes if they met Catherine's. "There's the little **rascal**!" he said, bending down as if pretending that Robert was crawling to him instead of his mother. The child made a sharp turn away from Johnson, provoking a burst of laughter from the others in the room.

---

vulnerability [ˌvʌlnərəˈbɪlətɪ] Verwundbarkeit **to monitor** [ˈmɒnɪtə] überwachen **rascal** [ˈrɑːskl] Frechdachs

Exercise 10: Johnson and Catherine

Match the sentence halves so that the statements make sense.

1. Johnson felt excited...	☐	**a.** the woman Johnson nearly married.
2. Catherine was honoured...	☐	**b.** how beautiful Catherine was.
3. Johnson was afraid...	☐	**c.** to see Catherine.
4. Catherine resembled...	☐	**d.** to welcome Johnson to her house.
5. Johnson noticed...	☐	**e.** looking at Catherine too often.
6. Johnson hadn't realized...	☐	**f.** of losing those he loved.
7. Catherine hadn't seen Johnson...	☐	**g.** Catherine's dimples.
8. Johnson avoided...	☐	**h.** since the visit to the *Duck and Drake.*

They sat for an hour discussing the house and the surrounding area, who the neighbours were and which ones were influential. Their closest neighbour, a government minister, lived just beyond the river at the end of the property, and the governor of the Tower of London had a large **plot** of land not far away. *A government minister and the governor of the Tower of London?* Johnson thought it an odd coincidence that someone like Catesby would have such neighbours. Was it possible, he wondered again, that Catesby had been **black-**

---

plot [plɒt] *hier:* Parzelle **to be blackmailed into doing sth.** [bi: ˈblækmeɪld ɪntə ˈdu:ɪŋ] durch Erpressung dazu gezwungen werden, etw. zu tun

mailed into organizing the plot by James's chief minister Cecil? If Catesby was a **pawn** of Cecil's, then history proved that he had managed to keep it a secret from the others until Guy Fawkes was caught on the night before the gunpowder was due to blow. If he had kept the secret from all the others, then why should he not be able to do the same with Johnson and Fanshawe?

A few months later it finally happened. The tunnel **succumbed to** the power and pressure of the River Thames. Its waters were now finding every weak point in the walls and leaking through into the basement, constantly widening the small cracks, turning every trickle into a steady stream. It would not be long before the water level rose above their heads.

Catesby ordered the men upstairs for an emergency meeting. Although Johnson had always known what would happen, he was also **distraught** at the sight. He, like the others, had invested a lot of time and energy in digging the tunnel, and he understood the sense of despair that now **engulfed** the room.

Catesby **paced back and forth** across the large living room as he waited for the others to settle down before addressing them. Johnson could see that he was deep in thought and wondered what he would have said himself if he had been in Catesby's position at this moment.

"Gentlemen, we have obviously encountered a serious **setback**

---

pawn [pɔːn] Bauer (*Schachfigur*) **to succumb to sth.** [sə'kʌm tə] etw. nachgeben **distraught** [dɪ'strɔːt] außer sich **to engulf** [ɪn'gʌlf] verschlingen **to pace back and forth** [peɪs 'bæk ən 'fɔːθ] auf und ab gehen **setback** ['setbæk] Rückschlag

in our plans, but we will not allow this to **dampen** our **resolve** or to cause divisions between us. This problem was unforeseeable and entirely beyond our control. We have to remain united. We can **bicker** and **whinge** all we like but it will get us nowhere. Our strength lies in our unity and our commitment to this mission. We must channel our frustration into constructive suggestions to overcome this disaster. Do we all agree?"

As the men all nodded, Percy stood up to speak. "Robin is right. We have to remain united, especially at a time like this. Remember, digging a tunnel was never our goal – our goal was to kill King James and his government. That's still our objective, isn't it? The flooding of the tunnel is just a disappointing setback in our strategy, but it doesn't change our objective. We simply have to put our heads together and come up with a new plan. **Despondency** won't help us now – what we need are ideas."

For more than an hour they discussed possible strategies for killing King James. Johnson sat back and listened; he didn't want to contribute too much in case he influenced the men to take a path that they might not have taken in his absence. They talked about poison, about shooting, about infiltrating the Court to stab him in the heart, to **strangle** him, to **suffocate** him. Few of the strategies seemed realistic to Johnson and those that did were given a **lukewarm** reception. Something was missing from each,

---

to dampen sb.'s resolve [ˌdæmpən / rɪˈzɒlv] jmds. Entschlossenheit dämpfen **to bicker** [ˈbɪkə] streiten **to whinge** [wɪndʒ] jammern **despondency** [dɪˈspɒndənsɪ] Mutlosigkeit **to strangle** [stræŋgl] erwürgen **to suffocate** [ˈsʌfəkeɪt] ersticken **lukewarm** [ˈluːkwɔːm] lauwarm

and each carried enormous risk. Furthermore, each strategy focussed solely on the King, and yet in order for their subsequent rebellion to be successful, they needed to attack his government at the same time. As he listened to the plotters, he felt as if he were standing in front of his students, waiting for them to come up with the answer that he, the professor, already knew. Several times the plotters were so close to the solution, but they kept missing it. They finally accepted that none of these strategies were **feasible**; gunpowder had to be used, and in large enough quantities to destroy the government. Two questions needed to be answered: where would the gunpowder be placed, and how would they get it there?

Johnson was taken completely by surprise when Fanshawe, who had remained silent throughout the discussion, now stood up to address the group. "A few days ago at the *Duck and Drake*, I overheard some merchants talking about small houses and apartments within the Parliament buildings. They said that each of these has its own cellar or storage room. I'm almost sure that one of the merchants said that he had managed to rent one of them. If it's true, maybe we could try to get one ourselves?"

"*Cellars*?" said Catesby, with a look of **bemusement**. "To *rent*? Directly beneath the Parliament? Why didn't you say this before?"

"Well, some of the other ideas seemed rather promising at first so I didn't really think of it until just now."

"Peter, my friend, if what you are saying is true, it would be the answer to our prayers. Percy, you have contacts at the

---

feasible ['fi:zəbl] durchführbar **bemusement** [bɪ'mju:zmənt] Verwirrung

Royal Court. Can you please make some discreet enquiries?"
"Of course, Robin. It may take a little time but I'll find out."
"Thank you. In the meantime, would everybody else please remain calm and try to stay positive. You should all spend every waking moment thinking of alternative strategies. We cannot rely on this lead until we know for sure that it is a **viable** option. We will meet again when Mr Percy has some news to report."
The plotters left the house for the last time. Catesby told Johnson and Fanshawe that he had some business to attend to, and would see them back at the house for supper. When he had moved a safe distance down the road, Johnson turned on Fanshawe. "You **imbecile**, Fanshawe. What in the name of God did you think you were doing in there?"
"Excuse me? What was I doing in there? I was making some useful suggestions, which is more than you can say for yourself. Would you mind telling me what the hell you are talking about?"
"Fanshawe, you complete idiot, have you lost your senses? You just told them about the cellars beneath Parliament. Now, thanks to your meddling, we'll never know how they resolved this crisis for themselves. Have you forgotten why we're here? We're here to find out what happened, not to help them to solve their problems. They would have found out about the cellars by themselves. For God's sake, Fanshawe, that's how *you* know about it! Our job – and remember, it is a job, not some kind of exotic holiday – is to observe and record, nothing more. We are scientists, we are

---

viable ['vaɪəbl] durchführbar **imbecile** ['ɪmbəsiːl] Idiot

investigators, we are not co-conspirators. We don't get emotionally involved and we don't allow ourselves to be affected by what we see. Try to remember that, would you?"

Fanshawe lowered his head for a brief moment and then stared directly at Johnson with a look of intense **hostility**. "You wouldn't be here if it wasn't for me. Try to remember *that*, would you?"

Exercise 11: What would have happened if things had worked out differently? Hypothesize about the past.

e.g. Fanshawe told the plotters about the cellar rooms. They didn't find it out for themselves.

If Fanshawe hadn't told them about the cellar rooms, they wouldn't have found it out for themselves.

Make similar hypotheses using the following facts.

1. The plotters needed a different strategy. The tunnel flooded.

______________________ if ______________

______________.

2. Fanshawe didn't remain emotionally detached. He told the plotters about the cellar rooms.

If ______________________________,

______________________.

---

hostility [hɒ'stɪlətɪ] Feindseligkeit

3. Fanshawe and Johnson had an opportunity to infiltrate the group. Catesby's son fell ill.

_______________________ if _______________

_______________________.

4. Johnson was a famous historian. He was asked to travel back to the seventeenth century.

If _______________________________________,

_______________________________________.

5. Johnson's mother died tragically. He vowed never to love anybody again.

If _______________________________________,

_______________________________________.

6. The British government established the Department of Historical Truth. The British lost the Taiwan War.

_______________________ if _______________

_______________________________________.

They walked in silence for fifteen minutes, neither man willing to **ease the tension** between them by making a friendly gesture of **reconciliation**. As they approached the

---

to ease the tension [iːz / ˈtenʃn] die Lage entspannen **reconciliation** [ˌrekənsɪlɪˈeɪʃn] Versöhnung

area that they knew as Leicester Square, a large crowd had gathered, perhaps two or three hundred noisy and excited people, **jeering** and shaking raised **clenched** fists at four men standing on a wooden platform in front of them. Two of the men looked out across the square, perhaps scanning the crowd for a friendly face or a sympathetic glance, while the other two stared down at their shoes, resigned to their fate and mumbling to themselves; Johnson assumed they were deep in prayer. Thick ropes needlessly bound their hands and feet; if their tortured and bloodied bodies had been free to struggle, they would hardly have had the strength to take a step without collapsing. Johnson and Fanshawe pushed their way through the hostile crowd to a spot five metres from the platform. This was the first time they had come across a public execution, and Johnson found himself morbidly fascinated. As the **executioner** placed a **noose** around the first man's neck, Johnson noticed that he, like the other three, wore an Agnus Dei, a small oval disc made from the wax **remnants** of an Easter candle blessed by the Pope. Such symbols were all the evidence the crowd would need to know that these men were not only Catholic priests, but that they were **traitors**, Papist agents loyal to the King's enemy – Pope Clement VIII. Johnson knew that there would be more to this spectacle than the hanging itself. When a priest was convicted of treason, the **penalty** was an absolutely horrific death, one that even the most twisted of minds would find hard to imagine.

---

to jeer [dʒɪə] höhnen **clenched** [klentʃt] geballt **executioner** [ˌeksə'kju:ʃənə] Henker **noose** [nu:s] Schlinge **remnant** ['remnənt] (Über)Rest **traitor** ['treɪtə] Verräter **penalty** ['penltɪ] gesetzliche Strafe

Johnson felt nervous as the crowd became increasingly noisy, driven to a **frenzy** of anger and expectation when the local sheriff read out the condemned men's names and their crimes. He watched reluctantly as the first priest was forced to slowly climb a few wooden steps, which were quickly kicked away to loud cheers from the crowd. The three other priests kept their heads down when their friend's face turned a patchy shade of reddish-violet as instinct forced the struggling man to gasp for air. After thirty seconds, the executioner climbed the steps and cut the rope, forcing the still-breathing priest to drop to the platform with a thud. He then raised a large sword, to cries of "Kill the traitor!" and "Death to Jesuit spies!" He swung the blade as hard as he could down on the priest's shoulder, splitting his **collarbone** and slicing through his internal organs. He then tore out the priest's heart and held it up to an ecstatic audience, shouting, "Behold the heart of a traitor!". Having been hung and drawn, the priest was now **quartered**. Each limb was hacked off, leaving only a heavily bleeding **stump** on the platform. Johnson knew that, as tradition dictated, the priest's arms and legs would later be posted on gates at the four corners of the city to send a chilling message to other Jesuit priests of the fate that awaited them.

Johnson turned to leave in shock, feeling sick at what he had seen; he couldn't bear to watch it happen three more times. He had seen a small group of people in the crowd who weren't cheering like the others and he assumed they must be Catholics. What were they thinking, he wondered?

---

frenzy ['frenzɪ] wilde Aufregung **collarbone** ['kɒləbəʊn] Schlüsselbein **to be quartered** [bi: 'kwɔ:təd] gevierteilt werden
stump [stʌmp] Stumpf

How did they **reconcile** their **pretence** at being Protestant with **adherence** to their true faith? What would they think if they knew what Robin and the others were planning? All the history books that Johnson had read spoke of the horror that engulfed the Catholic community in the wake of the plot's failure, but how would anybody know the true feelings of a persecuted community who had no choice but to **denounce** the plot after the event? It was obvious to Johnson that it would have been foolish in the extreme for anyone to disagree with the **Archpriest** Father Blackwell who denounced the plot after it failed as "intolerable, **uncharitable**, scandalous and desperate".

"Well," said Fanshawe, after they had made their way through the crowd, "what was that you said about not allowing ourselves to be affected by what we see? Animals aren't treated like that, Johnson. It's disgusting. It's hardly surprising that Catesby and the others are doing what they're doing. Those men aren't terrorists, they're simply trying to put an end to this **barbaric lunacy**. Tell me, what would you have done **if you were in their shoes**? Would you stand around and watch priests being slaughtered like **cattle** and do nothing about it? Sometimes I wonder, Johnson, whether you're really following the rules, or whether you're just a bitter and cold-hearted man."

---

to reconcile ['rekənsaɪl] versöhnen **pretence** [prɪ'tens] vorgetäuschtes Verhalten **adherence** [əd'hɪərəns] Festhalten
to denounce [dɪ'naʊns] denunzieren **archpriest** [ˌɑːtʃ'priːst] Erzpriester **uncharitable** [ˌʌn'tʃærətəbl] unbarmherzig **barbaric** [bɑː'bærɪk] barbarisch **lunacy** ['luːnəsɪ] Irrsinn **If you were in their shoes...** [ɪf 'juː wɜː ɪn ðeə ʃuːz] An ihrer Stelle... **cattle** ['kætl] Vieh

Johnson didn't answer him; he just quickened his pace, walking ahead of Fanshawe with his hands in his pockets and his head down.

Six

With the tunnel now abandoned, Johnson suddenly found himself with all the free time he had secretly wished for during the endless days of digging. It was a welcome change; he had seen and learned much, and needed time to **regain** his energy and reflect on his experiences. He was also desperate to get away from Fanshawe for a while. He was hurt by Fanshawe's comment after the execution and troubled by the possibility that there may have been a measure of truth in what he had said. He wondered if perhaps it was easier for him to **obey** the rules of their assignment; emotional detachment had been a dominant theme in his life since the death of his mother, and had been strengthened after Ruth had left him. Where he had once considered such detachment an **obstacle** to conducting a healthy relationship, it was now not only a great **asset**, but a primary *requirement* of the job. Despite this, Fanshawe's comments had forced him to think that if he was incapable of empathizing with the plotters – if he couldn't see things from their perspective on an emotional level – could he ever really get to the heart of it all? He wondered if he had ever really understood what history was about? Could he ever really unravel the truth, in its deepest, most human sense, behind the Gunpowder Plot?

---

to regain [rɪ'geɪn] wiedererlangen **to obey** [ə'beɪ] gehorchen
obstacle ['ɒbstəkl] Hindernis **asset** ['æset] Vorzug

On a chilly morning some six days after the execution, Johnson came down the stairs at Catesby's house to find Catherine alone in the dining room. Robin had left earlier on horseback with a pack of hounds to go hunting for the day, she told him, and would not return until late in the evening.
After breakfast, Catherine invited Johnson to join her for a walk in the grounds. She told him that she loved to get out of the house in the mornings to clear her head. Sometimes she would take long walks through the **pebble-strewn** paths that were **shielded** from the summer heat by rows of overhanging trees. Occasionally she would step off the path to pick a flower or chase a butterfly. On other days she might ride across their land to the river that formed the **boundary** with their nearest neighbour, or spend an hour or two tending the vegetable garden. Johnson asked her whether she would not prefer to go alone as this was the time that she usually set aside for herself.
"Believe me, Dr Johnson, I spend enough time alone. I would be delighted to have some company."
"That is a very **tempting** offer, Mrs Catesby, but I feel it my duty to warn you that my stories are painfully boring and my jokes are about as funny as the plague."
Catherine laughed as she took his arm and directed him down the hall and out of the back door. "Well, Doctor, my choice of walking companion is a little limited at present,

---

pebble-strewn ['peblstru:n] mit Kieselsteinen bestreut **to be shielded from sth.** [bi: 'ʃi:ldɪd frɒm] von etw. abgeschirmt werden **boundary** ['baʊndərɪ] Grenze **tempting** ['temptɪŋ] verführerisch

so I'll just have to suffer your **tedious** tales until I receive a better offer."

Exercise 12: Put the following nouns into the appropriate gaps. The first one is done for you.
(time, truth, guilt, practice, lie, gardens, space, personality, sound, story)

As Catherine showed Johnson the **1.** _gardens_____, **lanes**, trees, plants, and **hedgerows** she knew so intimately, he told her about his life in the North, about his imaginary brothers and sisters, about a house that he didn't own, and a medical **2.** ____________ that didn't exist. It was a story generated **at random** by a computer in the twenty-first century, which he modified here and there to fit the needs of a given situation. Although he had rattled the **3.** ____________ off a dozen times before, he felt a **pang** of **4.** ____________ now that he was telling this **5.** ____________ to Catherine. He wanted to get to know her, and he wanted her to know something about him, but there was almost nothing of **6.** ____________ that he could tell her. He tried to slip in some honest but uninter-

---

tedious ['tiːdɪəs] langweilig **lane** [leɪn] Gasse **hedgerow** ['hedʒrəʊ] Hecke **at random** [ət 'rændəm] zufällig **pang** [pæŋ] Stich esting facts whenever possible – his favourite tree was the oak, his favourite colour was blue – and he allowed his real **7.** ______________ come through as much as possible, but when she asked what his favourite food was, he couldn't tell her it was Japanese; when she asked what he liked to do in his spare **8.** ____________, he couldn't tell her that he was the **chairman** of his local flying club, and that just as she loved to wander through the woods, he loved to wander through the skies. He longed to tell her what it felt like to fly through the air faster than the speed of **9.** ____________, shooting along on a bed of clouds and then quickly dipping to race over mountains and valleys, rivers and oceans. He wanted to tell her about his recent **10.** ____________ flight, how it was finally becoming **affordable** for ordinary people to take trips out of the atmosphere and to **orbit** the planet in under an hour. He would have loved to describe to her what it was like to see the Earth from such great heights, a perspective that until recently had been reserved for God himself.

---

chairman ['tʃeəmən] Vorsitzende(r) **affordable** [ə'fɔːdəbl] erschwinglich **to orbit** ['ɔːbɪt] umkreisen

"Why aren't you married, Anthony?"
The question came so quickly and without warning that Johnson was **taken** completely **off guard**, but he knew that in order to answer it truthfully, he would not need to lie about where he really came from. This time, the lie would be avoiding the truth that Fanshawe had come so close to **exposing** the day before. "Marriage, Catherine, is an institution for either the very brave or the very responsible. I'm afraid I have neither of those qualities. And besides, when you wait too long, you find that all the best women are already taken."
Catherine smiled and lowered her head as Johnson gave her a friendly nudge with his elbow and exaggerated a twitch of his face, making sure some **ambiguity** remained in his comment. He hoped that she wouldn't be able to tell whether his little wink was meant to emphasize the compliment or suggest that he was simply fooling around in order to prevent this particular topic of conversation from going any further.
Johnson's early-morning walks with Catherine quickly became the high point of his days at Catesby's house. At dinner each evening, he had to fight the urge to stare across the table at her, and felt a rush of excitement at the thought that next morning he would be alone with her again. Robin was aware of how much time they were spending together but he didn't seem the slightest bit concerned or suspicious. He had told Johnson to spend his time as he pleased, although, he had said, it remained a mystery how a man of

---

to be taken off guard [biː teɪkn ɒf 'gɑːd] auf dem falschen Fuß erwischt werden **to expose** [ɪk'spəʊz] bloßstellen **ambiguity** [ˌæmbɪ'gjuːətɪ] Vieldeutigkeit

Johnson's position and learning could have no interest in hunting. On a chilly autumn morning in October, Johnson and Catherine walked further than ever before. The conversation flowed so easily between them that they hardly noticed the time passing and were both taken aback when they realized that they had reached the river. They sat down on the bank and looked out at the swans and ducks floating peacefully past.

"I'm glad you're staying with us, Anthony."

"So am I, Catherine."

"I was very lonely before you arrived."

"But you have Robin and Robert and..."

"I don't have Robin. Nobody has Robin except Robin. He's too caught up in whatever it is he's doing to care about me or Robert. He likes to pretend that we're happy together when we're in public, but we live in two completely separate worlds. I think he sees me as a kind of necessary **appendage** for social functions. He cares more about saving the world than saving his marriage. He cares more about strangers than his own family."

"Oh, come, I'm sure that's not true."

"It is. And I don't care any more. I stopped caring about Robin a long time ago, when I realized that he was never going to care about me. I was so naive, Anthony. I thought that there could be some affection in a marriage, that even though it's really about two families making an economic commitment to each other there could still be some **fondness** between the two people who married each other. How stupid I was!"

"Catherine, I ... "

---

appendage [əˈpendɪdʒ] Anhängsel **fondness** [ˈfɒndnəs] Zuneigung

"Why are you so kind to me? Sometimes I think you're from another world, Anthony. You treat me like an equal, you listen to what I say, you even seem to enjoy my company. That's not normal for a man of your class and upbringing."

"But surely Robin also ..."

"Shhh ... " Catherine put her hand to Johnson's lips. "I don't want to talk about Robin anymore. I'm not here with him. I'm here with you."

Catherine moved towards him with an unexpected and **unnerving** confidence, paralysing Johnson with a fear he hadn't felt since he was a teenager. As her fingers slid down towards his chin, she gently stroked his beard and pulled his face to hers. Their kiss was as magical and terrifying as anything he had ever experienced. It made him feel young and free and alive again. Here, in Catherine's arms and without having to speak, he could finally be honest and true, to himself and to her. Slowly and gently they lay back on the cold grass and made love to the sound of the river. Afterwards, they fell into a deep and contented sleep, waking only with the cold at nightfall.

Seven

Fanshawe, too, was happy to avoid Johnson as much as possible; the constant **nagging** about the rules was starting to **grate on** his **nerves**. He was sick and tired of being treated like a schoolboy and resented the condescending tone that Johnson often adopted towards him. He saw

---

unnerving [ˌʌn'nɜːvɪŋ] nervös machend **nagging** ['nægɪŋ] Nörgelei
to grate on sb.'s nerves [ˌgreɪt ɒn / 'nɜːvz] an jmds. Nerven zerren

Johnson as an equal and was irritated by this attitude that suggested he was somehow in charge on this mission. He had also begun to see that Johnson could be extremely **volatile**; one moment he was affable, warm, and gracious; the next he was in a **poisonous** and turbulent rage. The previous week, after Fanshawe had intervened in the strategy discussions, Johnson's face had turned an unnatural shade of red; his eyes had bulged with fury over the **bags** that had developed beneath them over the past few months. They had both lost a lot of weight and bright red blood vessels were now visible under the thin skin on Johnson's **protruding** cheekbones. His anger at Fanshawe had caused worm-like veins to rise to the surface at both **temples**, and his frown had been so deep that his thick black eyebrows had seemed as if they were joined together.

Despite Johnson's behaviour, however, it was he – Fanshawe – who had invented time travel. It was he who had opened up a world of opportunity for humanity through his scientific achievements. It was he who had turned the oldest human dream into a reality. So what if it was to be kept a secret? Who cared if he was never to be showered with **adulation**? He didn't need a Nobel Prize. He had no desire to have his back slapped in recognition by his so-called **peers**. They weren't his equals. Who else in history had matched his achievements? Copernicus? Galileo? Newton? For now, he simply longed for some freedom to explore this new world.

---

volatile ['vɒlətaɪl] launisch **poisonous** ['pɔɪznəs] giftig **bag (under the eyes)** ['bæg ˌʌndə ðɪ 'aɪz] Tränensack **protruding** [prə'tru:dɪŋ] hervorstehend **temple** ['templ] Schläfe **adulation** [ˌædʒʊ'leɪʃn] Lobhudelei **peer** [pɪə] Ebenbürtiger

On the day when Johnson and Catherine walked as far as the river, Fanshawe rose at dawn and left the house while the others were still sleeping. He walked quickly through the brisk morning air towards the centre of London, smiling and tipping his hat to strangers along the way. He was beginning to feel better, both mentally and physically; he **had slimmed down** considerably with the combination of the tedious diet he had been subjected to and the physical labour involved in digging the tunnel, and these days he walked with a little spring in his step. He could forget about the plot and Johnson and Smith and Catesby and all the others and simply wander aimlessly around his native city on an ordinary, bright summer day. After walking for an hour, it occurred to Fanshawe that they had only been in the seventeenth century for less than three months. They had left in May, and he worked out after a few moments that today must be the fifteenth of August, his birthday. As he passed the front door of a busy bakery, he waved to the people inside, feeling giddy and light-headed at the thought that he would be born exactly four hundred years later to the day, in 2004.

He headed south, crossing the Thames just beyond St Paul's Cathedral, and walked slowly along the south bank of the river. Fanshawe was by now used to the filth and smell of the city and on this morning he almost embraced it; he was a little tired of feeling like an alien in a strange world and felt the need to integrate himself more into his surroundings. The sun was now warming his face and his spirits had lifted considerably since the stress of the previous week. He **trudged** along the dirt tracks that ran parallel

---

to slim down [ˌslɪm ˈdaʊn] abnehmen **to trudge** [trʌdʒ] (mühsam) stapfen

to the river, randomly turning into side lanes where bakeries and **brothels** sat side by side. Although it was early, the area was already busy with activity; traders had erected their stalls, and people were out buying bread, meat, and vegetables for the day.

Fanshawe entertained himself by trying to guess which area he was in, which streets he was walking down, whether they existed in the world that he knew, or whether they had long since vanished. Walking under a stone bridge, he soon passed by the Clink Prison; he had visited this place as a museum in his childhood and once or twice as an adult. He remembered it having something of a theme park quality, a surreal place in which it was impossible to truly imagine the horror of what it must have been like to be a prisoner there. This bright August morning in 1604, however, it was still being used as a jail. How many Catholics, he wondered, were at that moment chained to the damp walls of dark and terrifying **dungeons**, having committed no greater crime than refusing to attend Protestant church services? He tried to push the thought out of his mind; today was not a day for thinking about these issues. There would be plenty of time for that in the coming months. Walking east now, he turned slightly away from the river and soon found himself standing before a circular building that looked vaguely familiar. He walked around it, admiring the thick, whitewashed walls that drew attention to the black wooden beams that gave it both support and elegance. From where he stood, he couldn't see that the **thatch** on top of the building did not cover the entire roof, but only a thick circular portion close to the walls.

---

brothel ['brɒθl] Bordell **dungeon** ['dʌndʒən] Kerker **thatch** [θætʃ] Strohdach

As he came to the front of the building, he spotted a wooden plaque hanging outside. Three bright red words had been painted onto it: The Globe Theatre. He went inside, following the sound of voices coming from the centre of the theatre. Standing quietly at the back, Fanshawe watched in **awe** as William Shakespeare directed his actors in a **rehearsal** of *Troilus and Cressida*. He thought how wonderful it would have been to speak to the great playwright, but he was now deep in concentration and would surely not have appreciated the distraction. In any case, he wondered, what would he have said to Shakespeare? Fanshawe stood silently in the shadows, thinking back to what Johnson had told him about Shakespeare's connection to the world of the plotters; how he came from the same part of the country as them; how his father and Catesby's father had been friends; how his mother came from a well-known Catholic family; how Shakespeare moved in the same circles as the plotters in London, often meeting other writers such as Ben Jonson and Sir Walter Raleigh at the Mermaid Tavern on Bread Street, where Catesby, Percy, Fawkes, Wright and Wintour also regularly met. The men were not close friends of Shakespeare, but he knew who they were and they knew of him long before his fame and success. Johnson had told Fanshawe that King James had decided to patronize Shakespeare's theatre company just the previous year. The King's Company, as it came to be known, was fortunate to have the monarch's patronage; most of London's theatres had been closed down due to the continuing **prevalence** of the plague, but the Globe had managed to remain open.

---

awe [ɔː] Ehrfurcht **rehearsal** [rɪˈhɜːsl] Probe **prevalence** [ˈprevələns] Vorherrschen

Fanshawe left and moved back towards the river, continuing his walk eastward. He passed the homes of some of the city's poorest residents, often hearing the heart-breaking moans and cries of those sick with the plague as rats **scurried about** under doorways that had been marked with paint by the city authorities to warn the public that infected people lived here. What a pity, he thought, that these people had to suffer so needlessly. If only they knew what little effort was required to stay healthy. He almost felt **compelled** to run into one of these stinking **shacks** and give its residents an impromptu lecture on the causes of the plague and the benefits of hygiene. Before long, he saw the imposing walls of the Tower of London. Again he was reminded of the **plight** of the Catholics; the Tower was a maximum security prison, reserved for the most hardened criminals, especially those who posed a threat to the monarchy. Foremost amongst these were, of course, Jesuit priests, who died in countless numbers inside its cells, in its courtyards, and beyond its walls.

Exercise 13: Match up these locations with the corresponding description.

1. The Globe Theatre
2. St Paul's Cathedral
3. The Clink Prison
4. The Catesby residence
5. The Tower of London
6. The Mermaid Tavern

---

to scurry about ['skʌrɪ ə'baʊt] hin und her huschen **compelled** [kəm'peld] gezwungen **shack** [ʃæk] Hütte **plight** [plaɪt] Notlage

a. ☐ A famous place of punishment where people who posed a threat to the monarchy were kept.
b. ☐ A place of punishment where suspected Catholics were held.
c. ☐ A circular building with white-washed walls.
d. ☐ A place where **refreshments** were sold, frequented by famous writers.
e. ☐ A **place of worship** near the Thames.
f. ☐ A building near the lands of the Governor of the Tower of London.

And suddenly Fanshawe began to realize that, no matter how hard he tried, he could not simply take a break from the plot; he was surrounded by reminders of the injustices that had led Catesby and the others to their actions. He sat down opposite the Tower and stared at it for almost an hour. Instead of emptying his mind of thoughts of the plot, he now thought about it with a greater intensity and clarity than ever before. The whole experience up to now had been something of a surreal novelty, a stage play like one of Shakespeare's dramas – but one in which the cast of characters and the plot were known in advance. **For all intents and purposes**, it was merely an extension of the virtual reality training that they had received at the Department of Historical Truth. But witnessing the brutal execution had brought home to Fanshawe how real the situation was; it explained the intensity of the plotters' beliefs and the lengths to which they were willing to go to create a more just and tolerant England. He

---

refreshment [rɪˈfreʃmənt] Erfrischung **place of worship** [ˌpleɪs əv ˈwɜːʃɪp] Gotteshaus **For all intents and purposes ...** [fər ˈɔːl ɪnˌtents ənd ˈpɜːpəsɪz] Im Grunde ...

enjoyed the company of Catesby and the other men, and the more he thought about their plight and the plight of all Catholics, the more he began to feel that what they were planning to do was justified under the circumstances in which they found themselves. In the world that he had come from, people took for granted the rights of minorities and people's freedom to express their thoughts, their opinions, and their religious beliefs. He had rarely thought about how those rights had been secured; it occurred to him now that it must have taken centuries of struggle against tyranny and persecution. Although people like Catesby and Fawkes were remembered in history as traitors and terrorists, Fanshawe now thought that it was unfair and **over-simplistic** to apply modern values to a set of circumstances that were so utterly different.

As he watched the King's horsemen guarding the gates of the Tower, he began to question the relationship between his former life and his present one. Why should the events and realities of 2055 be more important, more significant, or more real than those of 1604? What exactly was the relationship between the two? Why should his actions here submit to his responsibilities in the future? The Department of Historical Truth was part of a state structure that favoured the status quo; of course they didn't want to change history. To change the past would be to risk their current position. It was easy for Smith to talk about historical objectivity; as long as the past stayed the same, she, the Department, the government, and the monarchy in 2055 remained unthreatened. As Fanshawe stared at the walls of the Tower of London, he wondered whether loyalty should be dictated by accident of birth or the opportunity to follow one's conscience when-

---

over-simplistic [ˌəʊvəsɪmˈplɪstɪk] zu grob vereinfachend ever such an opportunity arose. The fact that modern Britain had recently become a relatively tolerant place did not excuse its cruel past. If an opportunity arose to prevent or at least **mitigate** that cruelty, would this not override any future responsibilities? Should he not act according to his values wherever he found himself? These thoughts disturbed Fanshawe as he crossed back over the river and began to walk north through the city. Not wishing to return to Catesby's house too early for fear of meeting Johnson, he drifted about the city, getting lost in the alleys and lanes.

After an hour or so, he found himself emerging onto a broad **thoroughfare** that looked familiar. He soon realized where he was when he spotted Percy coming out of his house and descending the steps onto the street, accompanied by Fawkes. The men seemed delighted to see Fanshawe when he ran over to greet them; Percy smiled and slapped Fanshawe's back. "Well, if it isn't the good doctor himself! What brings you to these parts, my friend?"

"Little more than the need for some exercise and a poor sense of direction, I'm afraid, Tom, but it's a welcome surprise to see you both."

"And a most fortunate coincidence, wouldn't you say, Guido?"

"I surely would. Three pairs of eyes are better than two when an apartment and cellar under the House of Lords require examination."

Fanshawe's eyes opened wide in delighted surprise. "Are you telling me that you're going there right now to view the place?"

---

to mitigate ['mɪtɪgeɪt] mildern **thoroughfare** ['θʌrəfeə] Durchgangsstraße

Guy Fawkes slapped Fanshawe's back and smiled, adding under his breath: "Indeed we are, Peter. Come, join us. I imagine it will be most interesting to view the very spot from which our King's death sentence will be carried out."
When they reached the Parliament complex, Fanshawe was astonished to see so much activity. The Palace was not only the seat of government; it was also used for all kinds of commercial **enterprise**. He saw taverns, wine merchants, traders' stalls and even a baker's shop right within the complex. It occurred to him that the twenty-first century obsession with security had developed over hundreds of years as a result of the kind of action that he was now there to help plan.
Percy led the way to the back of the main building and down Parliament Stairs, a set of winding steps that led to a large open space called the Cotton Garden right next to the river. Here they met a sour-faced and foul-smelling old woman called Susan Whynniard who took the men into the small, one-roomed apartment that she owned within the complex. As she carefully examined Percy, Fawkes and Fanshawe with a look of dislike, she waved a finger at Percy. "I don't know what you expect me to do, Mr Percy. Mr Skinner has been renting this place from me for years now and Mrs Bright has all her **coal** stored below." With the mention of the existing tenants, Fanshawe knew that money, and not charm, was needed to persuade this **grumpy** old woman to rent them her property. He took out a bag of coins and handed a large sum of money to Mrs Whynniard.

---

enterprise ['entəpraɪz] Unternehmen **coal** [kəʊl] Kohle **grumpy** ['grʌmpɪ] missmutig

As she showed them the storeroom at ground level below the apartment, Percy pointed at Fawkes and introduced him to Mrs Whynniard as John Johnson, the name he would insist was his even after he was eventually captured in the storeroom where they now stood. "My servant here will be looking after the place until my wife arrives in London. He'll be sure to keep the place in good condition."

After successfully securing the **lease** for the sum of four pounds, plus a nice bonus for Mrs Whynniard to get rid of Skinner and Bright, the men went for a celebratory drink. The following Friday evening, Fanshawe arrived at the *Duck and Drake*, excited at the prospect of sharing the good news with the group. When they were settled, Guido told them that he had already moved into the Whynniard apartment and had started examining the storeroom in further detail. "Apart from Mrs Bright's coal, the room is full of old bits of furniture and crumbling **masonry**, and it's covered with layers of dust and dirt. It's got the air of an uninteresting and abandoned place – it's perfect." He took out a rough plan of the building that he had drawn up from his examination of the complex. "If you look at it from above, the parliament looks like the letter H, with the House of Lords occupying the upper floor of the **crossbar**, here." Guido then pointed to the lower part of the left-hand block, indicating the exact location of the apartment; it too was on the upper level, with the storeroom lying directly beneath at ground level. "The distance between the storeroom and the House of Lords is roughly

---

lease [liːs] Pachtvertrag **masonry** ['meɪsnrɪ] Mauerwerk **crossbar** ['krɒsbɑː] *hier:* Querstrich

thirty metres – easily close enough to cause serious damage."

Catesby could barely sit still with excitement. "This is perfect, *this is perfect*! Guido, how much space is there in the storeroom?"

"Enough to hold at least three tons of gunpowder. With the measurements I've made, I think there's plenty of space to hold about fifty **barrels**, maybe more."

"Good, that should be enough to destroy the entire complex. It's a pity the King will die so quickly – I'd like him to survive just long enough to realize what has happened."

Although Fanshawe knew that Johnson would **disapprove**, he couldn't resist joining in the conversation. He, Fanshawe, had suggested renting the apartment, and he had been there when Percy managed to secure the lease. He was beginning to feel that he was as much a part of the conspiracy as the others. If Johnson didn't like it, that was his problem.

"So, where exactly do we get the gunpowder? I thought the government had a monopoly on it?"

Guido smiled, giving Fanshawe a **pitying** look that suggested he should know better. "In theory, maybe, but when you know the right people, gunpowder is as easy to come by as a **loaf** of bread. Every soldier carries gunpowder as part of their equipment – they even have their wages reduced to pay for it. Naturally they're not too happy about this, so to make a little extra money, they try to sell their **supplies**. And you know all those merchant ships you see going up and down the river? Every one of them carries a

---

barrel ['bærəl] Fass **to disapprove** [ˌdɪsə'pruːv] missbilligen **pitying** ['pɪtiɪŋ] mitleidsvoll **loaf** [ləʊf] Laib **supplies** [sə'plaɪz] Vorrat

substantial stock of gunpowder, and for the right price. They don't mind **offloading** a little weight."

Catesby told the men that each of them would have to discreetly purchase as much gunpowder as possible in small quantities, using different sources. They would store it at his house in Lambeth, from where Fawkes would take it across the river, unloading it at the Cotton Garden and taking it into the storehouse. There it would be covered with coal and firewood until the time was right.

"Gentlemen, Parliament is due to reopen on the seventh of February. Our beloved king now has less than two months to live."

Exercise 14: Remember!

"Remember, remember the fifth of November,
Gunpowder, treason and plot.
I see no reason why gunpowder treason
Should ever be forgot."

What are the facts about the gunpowder the plotters are using?

Mark the correct alternative.

1. The gunpowder will be stored *(thirteen/thirty)* metres away from the House of Lords.
2. There is enough space in the storeroom for at least *(three/thirty)* tons, or *(fifteen/fifty)* barrels of gunpowder.
3. The government *(actually/theoretically)* has a monopoly on gunpowder.
4. The money to purchase gunpowder for the soldiers' equipment is *(added to/taken off)* their wages.

---

to offload [ˌɒfˈləʊd] abladen

5. The soldiers frequently try to *(purchase/sell)* supplies of gunpowder.
6. Catesby wants the men to *(discreetly/openly)* purchase as much gunpowder as possible.
7. The gunpowder will be stored at *(Fawkes'/Catesby's)* house.
8. *(Fawkes/Catesby)* will ship it over the river to the Cotton Garden.

Eight

Johnson and Catherine had managed to keep their relationship a secret from everyone. Their morning walks were accepted as part of the routine at the Catesby house and Johnson was confident that neither Robin nor Fanshawe suspected a thing. He had agreed with Catherine that he should spend more time with Robin, to **quell** any suspicions her husband might have about the exact nature of the relationship between his house guest and his wife. This suited Johnson well as he also needed to spend time alone with Catesby to try to find out whether there could be any possibility that Cecil had blackmailed him into the plot. So far, he had found no reason to believe that this was true.

Johnson had told Catherine that he and Fanshawe were to become business partners with her husband, and that it would take a considerable time for them to find **suitable** homes in London. She had no reason to doubt this explanation and never questioned their presence in her home. Since her relationship with Johnson had begun to develop,

---

to quell [kwel] unterdrücken **suitable** ['suːtəbl] passend

she told him that she thought of little more than how they could continue it in such risky circumstances.

One cold, dark midwinter morning, Catesby and Johnson rode out for a day's hunting while discussing key figures in James's government who might be involved in directing the persecution of Catholics. Catesby began to complain bitterly about his own **father-in-law**, Sir Thomas Leigh, a Protestant and a loyal supporter of King James. "I'm sure that snake is wrapped up in James's plot against the Catholics, but I've never had enough evidence to prove it."

"What makes you say that?"

"Just listen to him for five minutes and you'll understand. The man is evil to the core. He's an **unprincipled** opportunist, always looking for ways to crawl up the political ladder."

Catherine too was a Protestant, although she rarely spoke to Johnson about religion. On the one occasion when the subject had arisen, she told him that religious issues only interested her as far as they affected her family, and since Robin had been released from prison seven years earlier, she had no reason to concern herself with the ongoing problems in the country. Her only concern, she told him, was the constant arguments between Robin and her father; she **dreaded** the evenings when Sir Thomas came for dinner. The talk of politics and religion inevitably degenerated into an argument between her husband and her father and usually ended with one of them walking out.

---

father-in-law ['fɑːðərɪnlɔː] Schwiegervater **unprincipled** [ʌn'prɪnsəpld] gewissenlos **to dread sth.** [dred] sich vor etw. fürchten

After Percy and Fawkes had shared the news about the apartment and storeroom with the other plotters, Catesby, Johnson and Fanshawe arrived home to find Sir Thomas sitting with Catherine in the living room. Catesby introduced the two house guests to his father-in-law as Bates served a round of drinks. Sir Thomas wore a persistent, weasel-like grin, and Johnson sensed immediately that this was a stubborn and **pugnacious** little man. He had to lean down to shake Leigh's hand, as the top of his head only reached to the height of the professor's chest. As Johnson stared at the white **sideburns** that stuck out from each side of Leigh's face like handles on a pot, he imagined the tiny knight being lifted by his **whiskers** into his chair at the dining table. Dinner that evening was intolerable for Johnson; he sat between the husband and the father of the woman he was falling in love with, and directly across from Fanshawe, to whom he hadn't spoken for days. He had a reason to avoid eye contact with every person at the table, and spent the better part of an hour staring down at his plate. He desperately wanted to look across at Catherine but felt sure that his true feelings for her would be revealed by a simple glance. He was tormented by the guilt of betraying Robin and although he tried to persuade himself that his actions were beyond his control, he knew this wasn't true. He felt guilty for lying to Catherine about his true identity, and guilty at the knowledge that one day he would have to return to the future. When that time came he would have to lie again.

When Johnson eventually peered up from his plate and glanced around the table, he realized that everyone present

---

pugnacious [pʌgˈneɪʃəs] streitsüchtig **sideburns** [ˈsaɪdbɜːnz] Koteletten **whiskers** [ˈwɪskəz] Backenbart

had at least one dark secret. He wondered if Catherine was hiding anything else from her husband and father, or possibly from Johnson himself? Could Leigh sit for dinner with his son-in-law and then go out into the world to **condemn** Catholics to torture and death? Was Robin acting alone or in the service of Cecil? And what about Fanshawe? Was it possible that he too had something to hide other than his futuristic origins? As dinner progressed, Johnson became aware that his position at the table was not accidental. He had been carefully placed to act as a **buffer** between Catesby and Sir Thomas, both of whom were clearly relieved not to have to address one another. Leigh directed most of his attention to Johnson, questioning him about recent developments in medicine. The professor did his best to answer politely without saying anything controversial or raising suspicions. Although his knowledge of medicine was limited, he had little difficulty in sounding authoritative and met Leigh's opinionated comments with circular responses worthy of a politician. He spoke for as long as he could, in order to avoid Catherine's eyes and to prevent Fanshawe from making up **elaborate** stories. Johnson prayed that Fanshawe wouldn't **get carried away** and tell them about the cure for the common cold, or, worse still, that Johnson had discovered it.

"Tell me, Doctor," said Leigh, rearranging the two cushions he sat on to allow him to see over the table, "what's your theory about this *plague* that everyone is so afraid of?"

"Well, Sir Thomas, as you know there are as many theories on this island as there are doctors … "

---

to condemn [kən'dem] verurteilen **buffer** ['bʌfə] Puffer **elaborate** [ɪ'læbərət] kompliziert **to get (got, got) carried away** [ˌget / gɒt / gɒt kærɪd ə'weɪ] die Kontrolle über sich verlieren

"Yes, but most of these doctors hardly know their arse from their elbow, am I right? Present company excepted, of course."

"It is true that even today there are some disappointing limits to our knowledge in the field of medicine, but …"

"Limits! You can say that again! I've been **incapacitated** with problems of the **bowel** for more than two years now and not a single doctor in this great city can provide me with relief."

"I'm sorry to hear of your troubles, Sir Thomas."

Leigh grunted as if to say he hardly expected Johnson to solve his problem, and that he would bravely struggle on without the help of the medical community. "I'll live. Anyway, where do you stand on this so-called *plague*?"

"Well, Sir Thomas," said Johnson enthusiastically, happy to have moved on from the subject of Leigh's bowels which **had diminished** everyone's appetite, "I must admit that the causes of the plague remain something of a mystery to me."

No sooner had Johnson given Leigh his disappointing answer than Fanshawe invited himself into the conversation. "I have a theory, Sir Thomas."

"Is that so? Do enlighten us, Doctor Fanshawe."

"I think the plague may be spread by infected **fleas**, which are carried by rats that come **ashore** from merchant ships. It seems to me that the people most affected by the plague are those who are in closest contact with rats, and there's a higher prevalence near the river than on the outskirts of the city."

---

incapacitated [ˌɪnkəˈpæsɪteɪtɪd] *hier:* geschlagen **bowel** [ˈbaʊəl] Darm **to diminish** [dɪˈmɪnɪʃ] verringern **flea** [fliː] Floh **ashore** [əˈʃɔː] an Land

Exercise 15: Put in the appropriate form of the verb "to be" (e.g. is, was, has been etc).

1. Sir Thomas said, "I ______________ incapacitated with bowel problems for three years now."
2. Fanshawe suggested that the plague may ________ spread by infected fleas which ________ carried by rats.
3. Johnson hoped that Fanshawe (not) ______________ indiscreet.
4. Johnson ____________ tormented by the guilt of betraying Catesby.
5. Johnson told Catherine that he and Fanshawe __________ to become business partners with her husband.
6. By the time Johnson met Catherine's father-in-law, Sir Thomas, he and Catherine ___________ lovers for several months.

Leigh paused for a moment without expression, as though giving deep thought to Fanshawe's theory before his unexpected response. "Ha! Nonsense, Doctor! Pure **quackery**! I've never heard such an absurd theory!"

---

quackery ['kwækərɪ] Quacksalberei

"Well," said Fanshawe, visibly taken aback by Leigh's **scornful** reaction, "it's just a theory, Sir Thomas, and of course I have no evidence. Perhaps you have a theory of your own?"

"You don't need a theory when you have the facts, Fanshawe." Leigh squinted and waved his finger in the air as a look of rage spread across his face. "I tell you this plague is the **wrath** of God brought upon us by the poisonous actions of those **accursed** Jesuits!"

While Johnson was relieved that nobody seemed to appreciate the enormous significance of what Fanshawe had just told them, Catesby's face was turning red with anger at Sir Thomas' words. "How dare you say that in this house! *How dare you!* You blame the Jesuits, others blame the Puritans, and yet this wicked disease does not discriminate among its victims. Do you think your beloved King is immune from the plague? Do you think he agrees with your learned diagnosis? His murderous actions are political, not religious. Even someone as **dimwitted** as you should realize that." As Catesby got up from the table and left the room, throwing his napkin at the table and directing a look of hatred at Leigh, Johnson recognized for the first time that Robin's **sincerity** could never be called into question. He was entirely committed to the plot.

Nine

Guy Fawkes **grimaced** as he stretched his arms over the edge of the boat and handed Peter Fanshawe a large

---

scornful ['skɔːnfl] höhnisch **wrath** [rɒθ] Zorn **accursed** [ə'kɜːsɪd] verflucht **dimwitted** ['dɪmwɪtɪd] dämlich **sincerity** [sɪn'serətɪ] Aufrichtigkeit **to grimace** [grɪ'meɪs] das Gesicht verzerren

wooden **cask**. At three o'clock in the morning it was too late for the drunks and too early for the traders to notice anything unusual about the two men. Had anyone passed by the river's edge at Lambeth that cold January morning, they would have assumed that the men were delivering goods to a merchant ship **bound for** the open seas later that day.

For three nights now, Fawkes and Fanshawe had loaded the barrels into the boat, taken them across the river to the Cotton Garden, and hidden them beneath piles of coal and firewood in the Whynniard cellar. A full moon **hovered** directly above the House of Lords, creating a sharp outline of the Parliament roof while helpfully illuminating the route that the men would take on their short journey across the river. Fawkes, easily the stronger of the two, pulled the heavy boat through the water, raising and dipping the oars with a silent, rhythmic determination. Fanshawe sat back, his arms stretched out over the barrels that rested peacefully to his left and right, listening to the **creaking** oars and the gentle **lapping** of water against wood. Black clouds passed across the face of the moon shortly before they reached the other side, gently **extinguishing** the reflection in the water that had lit their path. Fawkes pushed the oars forward and held them, slowing the boat down as they approached the bank. When Fanshawe had secured the boat with a length of rope to a wooden post at the river's edge, Fawkes began to unload the barrels, carefully passing them to Fanshawe one by one. As he held his

---

cask [kɑːsk] Fass **bound for** ['baʊnd fə] unterwegs nach **to hover** ['hɒvə] schweben **creaking** ['kriːkɪŋ] knarrend **lapping** ['læpɪŋ] Plätschern **to extinguish** [ɪk'stɪŋgwɪʃ] auslöschen

arms out, waiting for the fourth barrel, Fawkes stopped moving.
"Quiet, Fanshawe." Guido looked up in the direction of Parliament Stairs and then suddenly Fanshawe heard it too: the voices of several men and what sounded like dogs barking.
"Searchers," whispered Fawkes.
From the sound of the voices, the searchers were probably twenty metres from the top of the stone staircase. The sixty-six steps would take less than twenty seconds to descend. It was then forty metres across the Cotton Garden to where Fanshawe stood; the two men had less than a minute to act. If the searchers were looking for an escaped Jesuit, the men's barrels were an unlikely place to hide a Catholic priest, and probably too small. Fawkes and Fanshawe could continue offloading the barrels in the hope that the searchers would ignore them. Even if they approached the boat, they would see nothing unusual; Fanshawe thought they might raise fewer suspicions by continuing their work. On the other hand, he thought, they might wish to search the cellars. If so, they would take more of an interest in the content of the barrels and this was a risk they simply could not afford to take.
Forty-five seconds left.
The voices were getting louder now; the searchers had reached at the top of the steps.
"Fanshawe, give me the barrels, quickly, come on."
Thirty-five seconds.
Halfway down the steps now, the searchers stopped and looked directly at the two men at the river's edge. They blew their whistles and called out as the two large dogs began to bark at the dark figures. As Fanshawe strained his

arms to pass the second barrel to Fawkes, he caught his foot on the rope that tied the boat to the shore, almost dropping the barrel into the water.

Twenty seconds now.

"You there! By the boat. Stop right there!"

Neither man looked up. Fanshawe struggled with the last barrel, his arms and legs **quivering with** fear.

"They're coming, Fanshawe, *they're coming, come on! Hurry*!"

The searchers unhooked the **leads** from the dogs' collars, making them sprint forward with their teeth bared, ready to attack.

"In the name of King James, I order you to stop!"

Fanshawe could hear the **snarling** dogs behind him; they couldn't be more than ten metres away now. He leaped into the boat, forgetting to untie it from its **mooring**. Fawkes quickly picked up a large knife and cut the rope from inside the boat. As he pushed away from the shore with one of the oars, the larger of the two dogs leaped at them from the riverbank, **oblivious to the dangers** of leaving the shore. Fawkes instinctively lifted his oar, catching the dog on the chest, which **yelped** in pain as it fell into the icy water.

"Put your **hood** on, Fanshawe, for God's sake, don't let them see your face."

Fawkes looked as if he was using all his strength to get them as far away from the riverbank as possible, where the

---

to quiver with sth. ['kwɪvə wɪð] vor etw. zittern **lead** [liːd] Leine **snarling** ['snɑːlɪŋ] wütend knurrend **mooring** ['mʊərɪŋ] Verankerung **oblivious to the dangers** [ə'blɪvɪəs tə ðə 'deɪndʒəz] sich der Gefahr nicht bewusst **to yelp** [jelp] aufjaulen **hood** [hʊd] Kapuze

searchers now stood in silence, staring out at the two silhouettes floating away into the night. He rowed downstream, staying close to the shore so they would be out of view as quickly as possible; they would wait until the searchers had gone, and return to Lambeth when it was safe to do so.

They **had been stockpiling** gunpowder in Catesby's second house at Lambeth for almost three months now. After Fanshawe and Fawkes were almost caught, it was agreed that the men should deliver the gunpowder by day. Most boats unloaded cargo at the Cotton Garden during business hours, and they would be less **conspicuous** if they simply blended into the **bustle** of an ordinary day's activity. It would be considered perfectly normal for Percy's servant to be seen taking goods into the cellar beneath his apartment. Catesby suggested that they should transfer the gunpowder from the large barrels into smaller **firkins** – wooden casks about a quarter the size of a full barrel. He said they would be easier to move in and out of the boat quickly, but more importantly, they would attract less attention, as they were regularly used for transporting common goods such as beer and butter. Each man was responsible for making contact with soldiers and merchants; they were to buy up all the gunpowder they could find, making sure to purchase it in small enough quantities to avoid suspicion. This would take time and patience, and, importantly, money. Many of them lived off **inheritances** or **dowries**, and used their own resources

---

to stockpile ['stɒkpaɪl] einen Vorrat anlegen **conspicuous** [kən'spɪkjʊəs] auffallend **bustle** ['bʌsl] geschäftiges Treiben **firkin** ['fɜːkɪn] Fässchen **inheritance** [ɪn'herɪtəns] Erbschaft **dowry** ['daʊrɪ] Mitgift

whenever possible, but they now needed a fresh injection of cash.

At the meeting to discuss the events of the night before, Catesby introduced the men to Robert Keyes, a close friend and relative, who had a considerable fortune at his disposal, and who fully supported the plotters' objectives. He was brought into the group along with his **brother-in-law**, Ambrose Rookwood, who also **donated** a great deal of money to support the plot. Rookwood had organized many of the contacts for buying the gunpowder, and as such had become a valuable member of the group. In December, Catesby **had** also **enlisted** the support of his servant, Thomas Bates. He could now use Bates to deliver messages and provide logistical support from his home on the outskirts of the city.

Exercise 16: Find the odd one out.

1. a. grimace	**b.** smile	**c.** scowl	**d.** frown
2. a. firkin	**b.** cask	**c.** barrel	**d.** cash
3. a. keep	**b.** store	**c.** steer	**d.** stock
4. a. abandon	**b.** claim	**c.** leave	**d.** desert
5. a. eyes	**b.** cheeks	**c.** toes	**d.** lips
6. a. sensible	**b.** preposterous	**c.** stupid	**d.** silly

Following the introductions, Catesby's demeanour became grave as he told the group that he had an announcement to make. "I must tell you that I have some disappointing news, my friends. It appears that the continuing prevalence of the plague has forced the Parliament to **postpone** its opening until the third of October."

---

brother-in-law ['brʌðərɪnlɔː] Schwager **to donate** [dəʊ'neɪt] spenden
to enlist [ɪn'lɪst] gewinnen **to postpone** [ˌpəʊs'pəʊn] verschieben

His companions were **devastated**. They had invested so much time, energy, and emotion in the plot that to put it off now for almost eight months would surely test their resolve. Catesby tried to be positive. "My friends, we now have more time to concentrate on our plans for the period following the death of James. I will return to the Midlands and the North to cement our support and to finalize our plans for the rebellion. Guido can now return to the Low Countries to do the same."

Fawkes looked around the table at the **sombre** faces before him. "I will need some help on this trip, though. We can't force any of you to go, but I'd be most grateful if one of you would **volunteer to** make the journey with me."

On hearing Fawkes's **plea**, most of the men looked down at the table for fear of meeting his eyes and inviting a direct request. Such was the solidarity between the men now that no one wanted to be seen to avoid his responsibility. But most of the men had private lives: how would they explain an absence of several months to wives and children, most of whom knew nothing of the plot? Fanshawe knew how much it would have pained the men to let Robin down.

"I'll go."

Nine heads looked up in unison with the blank expressions of a column of drilled soldiers. As the men showed visible signs of relief, Fawkes smiled in appreciation.

"Thank you, Fanshawe."

---

devastated ['devəsteɪtɪd] am Boden zerstört **sombre** ['sɒmbə] düster **to volunteer to do sth.** [ˌvɒlən'tɪə tə 'du:] sich freiwillig melden, etw. zu tun **plea** [pli:] (dringende) Bitte

Ten

In the attic of the Tudor gatehouse that stood on the grounds of the Catesby **estate**, Johnson and Catherine lay naked in each other's arms under a soft quilt of duck and goose feathers. Three hours earlier, Robin had saddled up and started his long journey north in search of further support for the post-assassination rebellion. When Catesby suggested that Johnson, as a Northerner, might be a great asset on the trip, the professor complained of stomach problems, which he said would be made worse by continuous horse riding. As Tom Wintour offered to go in his place, Catesby didn't press the issue further, and wished the doctor a speedy **recovery**.

Catherine put her left elbow on the pillow and leaned her head in the palm of her hand, smiling in silence at Johnson as she **caressed** his cheek with her long black hair. "Tell me something about yourself that I don't know, Anthony. Just one little thing; one little insight into your mysterious character."

Johnson sat up quickly, suddenly in a panic that Catherine had discovered the truth and **was taunting** him, trying to make him admit his great secret to her. He relaxed a little when he saw that she was smiling, but the brief shock brought to the surface the two conflicting emotions that had caused him such pain throughout his life: his need for love, and the fear that it aroused in him. He thought of what Smith had said to him: *It is crucial that you do not form close, personal relationships with the people you meet in*

---

estate [ɪ'steɪt] Gut **recovery** [rɪ'kʌvərɪ] Genesung **to caress** [kə'res] liebkosen **to taunt** [tɔːnt] verspotten

the past. When Catherine had asked **awkward** questions before, Johnson had always managed an ambiguous **quip**, a witty remark that was neither wholly true nor completely false. Now, however, he felt the insecurity of an ordinary man falling in love, no longer able to hide behind a mask of humour, and desperately wanting to share at least some of the truth with Catherine. He was becoming tired of the acting and needed to be himself again, even for a short while. The prospect of being honest, however, made him feel nervous. He avoided her eyes and began to fiddle with the ring that Smith had given him. "I'm afraid."

"Of what?"

"Of losing you."

"Why?"

"My mother died when I was five years old." Johnson could see that she was puzzled by his response; it had been common for young people to die in the sixteenth century, and this hardly qualified as a character-revealing secret. "She was murdered."

"Oh, Anthony, you poor man. I'm so sorry. By whom?"

"By my father."

"What happened?"

"He pushed her away; he was too focussed on his work, and she turned to someone else for the love and affection she needed."

"That sounds familiar."

"One day he came home from work early and found them in bed together. He killed them both."

"What happened to him?"

"He was locked up and eventually died in prison."

---

awkward ['ɔːkwəd] unangenehm **quip** [kwɪp] witziger Einfall

"And you, what happened to you?"
"I was taken away and brought up by my grandparents – my mother's parents." Johnson felt as if a heavy weight had been lifted from him; he felt normal again for a few brief moments, and although his story was terrible and tragic, at least it was the truth. "But Robin would never ..."
"No, I'm sure he wouldn't. But we still have to be careful."
"I don't think we have to worry about Robin. He's too **absorbed in himself**. Ever since he was eight years old, when his father first went to prison, he's been obsessed with the persecution of the Catholics. And he's hardly spoken to me since the last time he got out of prison after that stupid man Essex persuaded him to join his ridiculous rebellion. He behaves as if it's a personal crusade for him, as if only he can liberate Catholics from their eternal suffering. All this **scheming** and plotting is sure to lead him straight back to prison, or maybe even to the **gallows**."
"So you know?" Johnson stared at Catherine in surprise. "I do have some intelligence, Anthony. Of course I know. I am married to the man, after all."
"Well, aren't you worried?"
"I gave up worrying a long time ago. This is who he is. It's what he does. It's defined him all his life. There's nothing I can say that will change his mind. For God's sake, we don't even talk about the weather any more, never mind his grand plans for political **upheaval**."
"But it must at least make you nervous?"
"Why? I've seen him off to prison and collected him from

---

to be absorbed in o.s. [biː əb'sɔːbd ɪn] mit sich selbst beschäftigt sein **scheming** ['skiːmɪŋ] Intrigen **gallows** ['gæləʊz] Galgen **upheaval** [ʌp'hiːvl] Umwälzung

prison on more than one occasion already. Worrying about it won't change anything."

"But this time it won't be prison. This time he'll be killed if he **fails**."

"What do you mean?"

"Well, if James survives he's hardly going to let Robin off with a prison sentence, is he?"

"I don't understand."

"If something goes wrong and Robin and the others are caught, they'll be executed. Surely that must give you some cause for concern, even if your marriage isn't exactly perfect?"

"What are you talking about, Anthony?"

"I thought you said you knew?"

"I know that Robin hides Jesuit priests and refuses to pay the fines imposed on him for his religion, and tries to convert Protestants, and pushes for change through sympathetic friends in Parliament. What do you mean 'if James survives'? What is Robin planning to do, Anthony?" As Catherine moved away from Johnson towards her side of the bed, Johnson realized that he had just made the biggest mistake of his life. He also realized that there was no way out of it now.

"Robin is planning to kill James."

"What are you talking about?"

"I know it sounds **outrageous**, Catherine, but it's the truth. Robin is orchestrating a plot to kill James and remove his government."

"What do you mean 'remove his government'? How exactly do you *remove* a government?"

---

to fail [feɪl] scheitern **outrageous** [aʊt'reɪdʒəs] empörend

Exercise 17: Put in the correct preposition.
(through, with, about, from, of, in, for (2x), out of)

He paused **1.** ______ a moment, wondering if there were any subtle or gentle way **2.** ______ describing their plans, whether there were any euphemism that might distance them **3.** ______ the **bloodshed** and horror that the others believed was going to take place.

"**4.** ______ several tons of gunpowder."

As Catherine climbed **5.** ______ the bed, she lowered her head into her hands as if she had suddenly got a bad headache. "Not again. Oh God, not again. I can't go **6.** ______ this again. How could he be so stupid? They executed Essex the last time. Robin was lucky to get away with his life."

He could no longer look her **7.** ______ the eye; he lowered his head, ashamed that this was the only response he could give her, and frustrated that yet again he couldn't tell her the full truth.

"And you, are you involved in this lunacy?"

"I'm sorry, Catherine. I thought you knew."

---

bloodshed [ˈblʌdʃed] Blutvergießen

"And Fanshawe?"

"Yes."

"So this is what your 'business partnership' is really

8. ________ then, is it? Mass murder? What kind of a business is that, Anthony? Tell me, I'd love to know. How could I have fallen **9.** ________ you? You, you ... *murderer*!"

Johnson jumped out of the bed, **pleading with** Catherine to listen to the full story, but she moved back towards the wall, shaking her head. "Get away from me, Anthony, don't touch me, *don't touch me!* I won't have the hands of a murderer on me. How could I have been so stupid? I thought you were different. I thought you were the first honest, caring man I had ever met. And what am I really to you? An entertaining distraction while you sleep under my roof and plan with my stupid husband to kill dozens of people. How dare you!"

"Please, Catherine, you must listen to me, I beg you."

"Why should I listen to you? What could you possibly say to me that would change anything? You plan to commit mass murder in cold blood. Surely there is no more to say?"

"Yes, there is, Catherine. There's a lot more to say. Listen to me. The plot is going to fail. I can't tell you how I know that, but it's true. Please believe me. It's definitely not going to happen."

---

to plead with sb. to do sth. ['pli:d wɪð / tə 'du:] jmdn. inständig bitten, etw. zu tun

"What do you mean? What are you talking about?"

"I wish I could tell you more, Catherine. There's nothing I want more in the world than to be able to tell you everything, but all I can tell you now is that you don't have to worry about all those people dying. It's not going to happen."

"How could you know that? Are you a spy?"

"No, I swear to you I'm not a spy, and neither is Fanshawe. It's extremely complicated, and I wish more than anything in the world that I could explain, but I can't. All I can tell you is that the plot is going to fail."

"You are a spy – you must be. How else could you know all this?"

"No, Catherine, on my honour, I am not."

"You're lying, you're lying! I hate you! Stay away from me."

As Catherine grabbed her clothes and ran out of the gatehouse, Johnson fell onto the bed and wept. It didn't occur to him that he had just put his entire mission at risk. He didn't think about the fact that someone as good and as kind-hearted as Catherine would do everything in her power to prevent such a terrible crime from happening. It didn't cross his mind that Catherine would have no choice but to stop it in order to protect herself and her son from the consequences. The plot, the whole mission, meant nothing to him at this moment. For now, all he felt was **remorse** at having caused Catherine such **anguish**, pain at having pushed her away, and shame at having kept the full truth from her once again.

---

remorse [rɪˈmɔːs] Gewissensbisse **anguish** [ˈæŋgwɪʃ] Qualen

Eleven

Johnson hadn't slept properly since Catherine had found out about the plot, and now that he had recovered from the initial shock he was terrified that he had put the whole mission **in jeopardy** by telling her. He spent endless days trying to work out how he might **salvage** the situation but had not been able to think of any **persuasive** argument that would convince Catherine that everything was all right. Even if he could persuade her that the plot was going to fail, how would he tell her that Robin would be shot dead soon afterwards? He knew that Catherine would not simply stay quiet and do nothing, letting the days and weeks pass until the men she now despised attempted to commit mass murder. Several times he had approached her in the hope that she would listen to him, but she refused to hear a word he had to say. Each time, he was torn between his loyalty to the mission and his love for her. He wanted to put her mind at ease and convince her that the plot would fail, not only in order to stop her from doing anything **rash**, but in the desperate hope that he might revive their relationship. Johnson had wanted to move out, to find a place of his own, and to get away from the tense atmosphere in the Catesby house, but he was sure this would arouse suspicions when Robin returned. He had also hoped, against the odds, that he and Catherine might find some middle ground, some space for reconciliation, but she refused to talk to him. Unless he was willing to explain how he knew that the plot would fail, she could not trust him. It was the key to his identity, she told him, and if he

---

in jeopardy [ɪn 'dʒepədɪ] in Gefahr **to salvage** ['sælvɪdʒ] retten
persuasive [pə'sweɪsɪv] überzeugend **rash** [ræʃ] unvorsichtig

couldn't, or wouldn't, tell her who he really was, there was little use in their wasting breath and energy on each other. They had developed a routine whereby they would avoid each other, sometimes for weeks at a time. Catherine would rise first, have her breakfast and take her daily walk alone. Johnson would wait until she had left and then leave the house, returning only after he knew that Catherine would be asleep. The atmosphere in the house had grown **unbearable**, and so Johnson was delighted when Catesby returned to London following his exhausting trip around the Midlands and the North. Robin looked so pleased to be home that he didn't seem to notice the icy tension between Johnson and Catherine that had persisted now for several months.

As soon as he returned, Catesby called a meeting at the *Duck and Drake* for the following afternoon; he had told Johnson that he had recruited more men into the group on his journey, and was eager to introduce them to the others. Returning to the old tavern **evoked** pleasant feelings of warmth and familiarity in Johnson. Walking through its heavy wooden doors was always a sort of homecoming. He hadn't set foot in the place for many months, and as soon as he entered the tavern and saw Blake behind the bar, he felt as much at home as he ever did back in the King's Arms in Oxford. It was in the *Duck and Drake* too that his sense of time was most **acute**. It was now almost fifteen months since their arrival, and yet he knew that when they returned to the Department of Historical Truth, only

---

unbearable [ʌnˈbeərəbl] unerträglich **to evoke** [ɪˈvəʊk] wachrufen
acute [əˈkjuːt] ausgeprägt

a few seconds would have passed. It was a confusing but **thrilling** concept, and one that he never **tired of** thinking about.

He often wondered whether he and Fanshawe would return after eighteen months in exactly the same physical state as when they left, and if they did, whether this would mean that time travel was effectively a way of living forever? Could you spend a lifetime at a particular place in the past, return to the exact point at which you left, and then return to spend another lifetime in the past before returning again? If you gained knowledge and wisdom in the past, what were the implications for education, science, philosophy, literature, music, art, technology, and politics? If a young person was sent to a point in the past, perhaps just thirty years earlier, could they spend years being educated and return with a lifetime of knowledge while still in their youth? What would the implications be for progress if a nation of teenagers had reached the highest levels of education possible? Could a government shut down its own education system, no longer requiring schools and universities? What would this mean for the economy? For the health service? For the energy sector and defence? On what platform would political parties stand if there were no more economic and social issues to resolve? If every child had the possibility of receiving the best possible education, who would be willing to work as cleaners, as rubbish collectors, as factory workers? Perhaps it wouldn't be possible to send all children into the past – how could they be expected to blend in without giving away their secret? Where

---

thrilling ['θrɪlɪŋ] aufregend **to tire of doing sth.** [ˌtaɪə əv 'duːɪŋ] müde werden, etw. zu tun

would the extra capacity come from in the schools of the past? Would the 'future children' become a despised minority group in the past, blamed for taking the places of worthy and legitimate children from that point in history? Would time travel thus become the preserve of the elite, reserved for only the wealthiest families who could afford such dramatic and exclusive treatment? Could time travel thus create further divisions in society, **exacerbating** the problems of a world already polarized between rich and poor? Could it ultimately be responsible for **fuelling** hatred and intolerance? Could future wars be fought because of time travel?

Exercise 18: Put in the appropriate noun.

e.g. educate ... *education*

1. hate ...
2. true ...
3. arrive ...
4. intolerant ...
5. tense ...
6. persecute ...
7. persuade ...
8. loyal ...
9. commit ...
10. rebel ...

---

to exacerbate [ɪg'zæsəbeɪt] verschärfen **to fuel** ['fjuːəl] schüren

Johnson tried to occupy his mind with these thoughts as he took a seat in their familiar corner at the back of the *Duck and Drake*, waiting for Catesby to introduce each member of the expanded group of plotters. There was Christopher Wright, known to his friends as Kit, a brother of Jack Wright. There was Robert Wintour, the elder brother of Thomas, who had a large fortune and had a reputation for **generosity**. There was John Grant, the man who had married the Wintours' sister, Dorothy. There was the volatile and **unstable** Francis Tresham, a first cousin of both Catesby and Tom Wintour; and there was the young Sir Everard Digby, the only member apart from Guy Fawkes and Thomas Bates who was not related to any of the others through blood or marriage. Catesby warmly welcomed each man and offered his profound thanks for their commitment and the risks they were taking in joining the group.

Fanshawe too was there, having earlier that day arrived back from his journey with Fawkes around the Low Countries. He seemed to be in high spirits, wearing a proud smile as Fawkes reported that they had managed to secure widespread support for the rebellion amongst exiled English Catholics and sympathetic Spaniards. As Johnson stared across the table, he realized how much he had missed Fanshawe and how much he needed him in order to be himself. There was nobody else he could talk to without having to worry about letting something slip about his true identity. At the same time, however, he couldn't help feeling a little jealous; while Johnson was the historian, the opportunity to travel and to witness so much of seven-

---

generosity [ˌdʒenəˈrɒsətɪ] Großzügigkeit **unstable** [ʌnˈsteɪbl] labil

teeth-century life had fallen to Fanshawe. Johnson knew that his painful experience with Catherine was magnifying his feelings of bitterness towards Fanshawe, but knowing the cause gave him little comfort.

When the meeting ended and the men sat around enjoying a few drinks, Fanshawe came over and sat beside Johnson and began to tell him about his extraordinary trip with Fawkes – how well he had been received everywhere they went; how people had treated him with **deference** and respect, and how he had been so impressive in enlisting support. Johnson had thought of Fawkes as a silent man but Fanshawe had seen a different side of him on the continent. He had taken naturally to the role of leader and had been loud and articulate in his speeches, persuasive and dominant in his discussions with the people whose help he eventually succeeded in enlisting. Although he listened attentively to every word, Johnson silently thought that Fanshawe could not possibly have had the capacity to understand or interpret the events that he had seen while travelling with Guido. He felt that a major opportunity to learn more about the events surrounding the plot had been lost. With the other men present there was a limit to how much Fanshawe could tell Johnson, and they agreed to wait up that evening until Catesby and Catherine had gone to bed in order to speak more.

While Johnson was surprised at how pleased he was to see Fanshawe again, he was also tormented by his mistake. He had always known that he would have to tell him eventually, but now that Fanshawe had returned from his trip with Fawkes, Johnson felt ill at the prospect of confessing

---

deference ['defərəns] Hochachtung

his blunder. Nevertheless, he decided that it was better to tell him sooner rather than later, and **resolved to** break the news to him later that night.

Robin was in high spirits back at his house that evening. During dinner he even managed to sound **magnanimous** when speaking to his wife. Catherine, however, did not appear quite so enthusiastic about her husband's return and his new-found **affability**. Johnson tried to imagine what she must be feeling, forced to sit amongst these three men with the knowledge she now had. Knowing about the murderous scheme must have made her feel sick at the thought of what they were planning to do. At the same time she might be afraid to mention it to her husband, afraid of what a man like that might do to ensure there were no risks and no loose ends. If he thought she could stand in the way of the plot, there was no **predicting** what he might do to make sure it succeeded. She must have felt sick too at the thought that Johnson and Fanshawe **were in on** it; all three of them, sitting there at the same table, enjoying a dinner of roast **pheasant**, in the knowledge that they would be responsible for the deaths of so many people in the coming weeks.

The moment she had finished eating, Catherine stood up, making some excuse about having to be up early the following morning, and went straight to her room. The men sat quietly for a few moments, sipping their drinks as they

---

to resolve to do sth. [rɪˈzɒlv tə ˈduː] beschließen, etw. zu tun **magnanimous** [mægˈnænɪməs] großmütig **affability** [ˌæfəˈbɪlətɪ] Leutseligkeit **to predict** [prɪˈdɪkt] vorhersagen **to be in on sth.** [biː ˈɪn ɒn] an etw. beteiligt sein **pheasant** [ˈfeznt] Fasan

listened to the sound of Catherine's footsteps on the stairs. Catesby, on the other hand, stayed up for hours, drinking heavily and telling the two men more about each of the new plotters. Although Johnson was exhausted, he had little choice but to wait for Catesby to **retire** first before he could speak to Fanshawe. He wondered where Catesby's energy had come from; he would normally have been sound asleep by ten o'clock.

Finally, at two o'clock in the morning, Robin announced that he was ready to sleep. Johnson stood at the bottom of the stairs and waited until he heard the door of Catesby's room close before he came back into the living room. Fanshawe was sitting in a large armchair near the fireplace, **sipping at** a glass of red wine as he tried to stay awake. Johnson was nervous as he came back into the room, not knowing how to **broach** the subject of his error. He was annoyed that he couldn't find the courage to come out and say it directly. After all, the sooner Fanshawe knew about it, the better. Instead, he talked around the issue for as long as he could, hoping that the right moment would present itself by chance, and that the confession would come out in a way that made his error sound unavoidable, or at least excusable. His admission would be made much more difficult by virtue of the fact that, in order to make it, he would have to tell Fanshawe about his affair with Catherine. This was the kind of personal information that neither man **had** ever **confided** to the other.

---

to retire [rɪ'taɪə] sich zurückziehen **to sip at sth.** ['sɪp ət] an etw. nippen **to broach** [brəʊtʃ] anschneiden **to confide** [kən'faɪd] anvertrauen

Exercise 19: Johnson is having difficulty communicating with Fanshawe. Complete the following "communications phrases".

1. to talk around	☐	**a.** a secret
2. to broach	☐	**b.** a blunder
3. to confide in	☐	**c.** slip
4. to mention	☐	**d.** an issue
5. to keep	☐	**e.** in passing
6. to confess	☐	**f.** an argument
7. to let something	☐	**g.** a subject
8. to put forward	☐	**h.** a friend

Johnson paced slowly around the room as he spoke, hoping his movement would keep Fanshawe awake long enough for the subject to arise naturally. "I'll say one thing for Robin, for all the ink that's been spilled about him there's no record in the history books of his capacity for drink."

"The man's talents are endless. I'd be jealous if I had the energy."

"It's a pity for him that his talents don't extend to good judgement."

"What do you mean?"

"I'm talking about the new men he introduced to us today – he now has his twelve disciples, and amongst them is one who will betray him."

"Tresham."

"Yes. At least, he's the prime suspect. We know that Lord Monteagle receives a letter on 26th October advising him not to attend the opening session of Parliament on 5th November. We don't know if that letter is authentic, or, if it is, who wrote it. We do know that Monteagle is Tresham's brother-in-law, and for many historians this is sufficient evidence that Tresham wrote the letter, but **I don't buy it**. I mean, why would Tresham *write* to his brother-in-law who lived within walking distance of his home? It would make much more sense to tell him in person. That way he could keep the information secure and discreet, and avoid the possibility of the letter falling into the wrong hands or being left behind as evidence. I think that Tresham probably told Monteagle in person, and that Monteagle then wrote the letter in order to distance himself from the plotters and to benefit politically after the plot was exposed, which he certainly did."

"What else do we know about Tresham?"

"We know that he lived a reckless and extravagant life in London throughout the 1590s. We know that he is unreliable, unpredictable, and highly volatile. We know that in his youth he brutally attacked an elderly man and his pregnant daughter who owed money to his father. And yet, for all his instability and the violence of his past, it seems that Tresham is torn between his loyalty to Catesby and the image in his mind of the **carnage** the explosion would cause. Even though he was among the last of the plotters to be recruited, he's central to the whole affair – I'm sure of it. We'll need to watch him carefully. If we **keep** our **eyes peeled** I'm sure we'll be able to add plenty to the files on him."

As the two men fell silent for a few moments, Johnson heard a noise from just outside the room like the sound of a chair that had accidentally been kicked, making a scrap-

---

I don't buy it. [aɪ dəʊnt 'baɪ ɪt] Das glaube ich nicht. **carnage** ['kɑːnɪdʒ] Gemetzel **to keep (kept, kept) one's eyes peeled** [ˌkiːp / kept / kept wʌnz aɪz 'piːld] seine Augen offen halten

ing noise against the stone floor. Standing up from his armchair, he shot Fanshawe a look of horror as he moved quickly but quietly to the door of the living room that led out into the hallway. There, leaping up the staircase two steps at a time, was Catherine. He turned around, rubbing the sweat from his brow as he moved slowly back to his chair. As he sat down, Fanshawe whispered, "What was it?"
Johnson knew he should have told Fanshawe the truth; he knew this was the perfect moment to explain his mistake and apologize, but the shame and guilt that had built up within him had clouded his judgement and stopped him from doing what he knew was right.
"Just the cat," he replied, "just the bloody cat."

Twelve

Johnson awoke in the dim half-light of early morning, with the first birds beginning to sing and the cold metal barrel of a hunting rifle pressed against his forehead. At first he thought he had a headache from the previous night's wine but as he gradually opened his eyes and saw Catesby standing over him, he began to realize what was happening.
"Get up."
"Robin, what the hell is … "
"Shut up. Get out of bed now, slowly."
"Robin, I don't understand, I … " Catesby turned the **rifle** around and smacked the **butt** of the gun against the side of Johnson's head, making his ears ring. He lost his balance and fell back onto the bed in pain.
"I told you to shut up. Now, once again, keep quiet and get

---

rifle ['raɪfl] Gewehr **butt** [bʌt] Gewehrkolben

on your feet." **Dazed** and disoriented, Johnson pushed himself up from the bed. He sat on the edge for a moment to regain his balance, holding his hand against his bleeding ear, and then slowly rose to his feet. As he lifted his head he saw Catesby standing directly in front of him, with the rifle pointed at his chest. Catherine was standing behind him, just inside the door of the room. She **was sobbing** heavily. Johnson opened his mouth to speak to her but stopped himself when he saw Catesby raise the rifle in warning.

"Come with me," said Robin, walking backwards towards the door.

Catherine left the room first; Robin reversed into the corridor, leaving enough space for Johnson to come out and walk in front. With the rifle now at Johnson's back, Robin ordered him into Fanshawe's room. "Sit on the edge of his bed and wake him up."

Johnson did as he was told, feeling rather odd as he gently nudged Fanshawe into **consciousness**, like a mother reluctantly waking a sick child. He sat up quickly and rubbed his eyes as Catesby turned the gun on him.

"You're spies, both of you!" Robin looked as if he were possessed; the veins on his forehead seemed ready to break through his skin and explode. His lower lip was quivering. "You intend to sabotage this plot and send me and the others to the gallows, don't you?" Johnson wanted to speak, to defend himself and Fanshawe, but was afraid that Robin would hit him again. "How very **convenient** that you were in the *Duck and Drake* the night my son was taken ill. How convenient, indeed! You followed us there,

---

dazed [deɪzd] benommen **to sob** [sɒb] schluchzen **consciousness** ['kɒnʃəsnəs] Bewusstsein **convenient** [kən'vi:nɪənt] praktisch

didn't you? Who told you about the plot? Come on, answer me. I want to know which one of them has betrayed me from the beginning. It couldn't have been Percy, I know that. Was it Jack? Or Tom Wintour? Surely not Guido?"

Neither man said a word in reply.

"Come on, damn you! I want to know! How could you do this to me? How could you pretend to be my friends and allies for so long, when behind my back you plan to see me hung, drawn, and quartered? How could you sleep in my house, eat my food, and drink my wine? How could you do it? *How could you do it?*" Catesby fired a shot into the ceiling. A cloud of dust and wood chips fell onto their heads.

Johnson realized that if they didn't try to defend themselves Catesby would be convinced of their guilt. He had to persuade him of their innocence. "Robin, please, give me one minute to explain. Kill us if you wish, but at least listen to us before you do. If you don't believe us, you will have lost nothing. But please listen to us. I swear to you on my mother's grave that we are not spies."

"He's lying, *he's lying!*" Catherine suddenly flew into a rage at hearing Johnson speak. One moment she was crying in the corner and the next she looked as ready as her husband to kill them. "*He's lying!*" She was screaming now, leaning towards Johnson with her hands raised and her fists clenched. Her eyes were closed in pain, and tears spilled down her cheeks. "You *liar*, Anthony, I heard the two of you talking tonight. You and Peter talked about the files that the government has on all these men, didn't you? Don't deny it. Government files, and what they said and didn't say. I heard you. You waited for us all to go to bed so the two of you could discuss your **surveillance** operation. Is that why you're staying here? Is that why you've been here all this time? To find out as much as you can about Robin and his friends? It makes me sick to look at you."

Johnson was the only one in the room who knew what Catherine was really asking him. He knew that there was more to her question than the others realized. *Is that why you're staying here? Is that why you've been here all this time?* He knew she was really asking him if that had been the only reason, or whether perhaps his other reason had been her, whether perhaps there was the slightest **glimmer** of hope that what they had was real and could be rescued. He couldn't bear to look at her; again he desperately wanted to tell her the truth. He wanted to tell her that his feelings for her were **genuine** and that he would happily give up all this nonsense for her if he could. But he couldn't.

"You told me that you knew the plot was going to fail, didn't you? Didn't you, Anthony?"

Catesby looked surprised. His wife obviously hadn't had time to give him the complete story. "Is that so? And how could you possibly know that it was going to fail unless you planned to sabotage it?"

Johnson knew that the evidence against them pointed in only one direction and began to think that there might be no way out of this. The worst thing he could possibly do, he knew, was to tell Catesby the truth. To tell him that they were on a mission from the future would have been the most ridiculously desperate and incredible story, and

---

surveillance [sə'veɪləns] Überwachungs- **glimmer** ['glɪmə] Schimmer **genuine** ['dʒenjʊɪn] echt

would probably have angered him even more. Even if he succeeded in convincing Catesby of their true origins, this would have even worse consequences; Catesby would demand to know the outcome, and would take pains to ensure that the plot succeeded.

"If only you would give us a minute, Robin, I'm sure we can sort this out. Catherine has obviously been imagining things. She has overheard pieces of conversations, and not knowing the context or the details, she has put two and two together and made five."

"Oh is that so, you intolerable, lying *bastard*!" Catherine ran at Johnson and slapped him across the face. He knew that the only way out of this was to plant a seed of doubt in Catesby's mind about the **credibility** of his wife's story. After all, she had told him in the middle of the night, having just overheard a late-night conversation from behind a closed door. If Johnson could only convince him that there was a reasonable possibility that she might have misunderstood the situation … Robin raised the gun again and pointed it directly at Johnson's face. The professor was terrified. He remembered what Fanshawe had told him back at the Department; that they had no idea what would happen if someone were to die in the past. He suddenly realized the seriousness of the situation – these could be the final moments of his life. He began **frantically** rubbing his silver ring and tried to think of something calming, something pleasant. The only image that came to his mind was his memory of being with Catherine by the river.

---

credibility [ˌkredəˈbɪlətɪ] Glaubwürdigkeit **frantically** [ˈfræntɪklɪ] hektisch

"Robin, please, it's true that I mentioned the plot by mistake to Catherine while you were away. I didn't mean to, it just slipped out. And as soon as I realized what I had done, I had to think of something to cover it up. I was afraid of how she would react. I couldn't think of anything quickly enough, so I just told her that it wasn't going to succeed; I hoped this would calm her down and **reassure** her that there was nothing to worry about. I didn't want her to worry about losing you over some plot that she knew nothing about."

Catherine was crying heavily again now; she leaned back against the wall and put both hands to her face, slowly sliding down until she was sitting on the floor. A sudden noise at the door startled Catesby, forcing him to swing around. Fanshawe, who had until this moment said nothing, suddenly leaped off his bed and struck Catesby as hard as he could on the back of his neck. He hit him again on the side of his head, and raised his knee into the small of Catesby's back. He then reached around and grabbed the rifle from him, giving him one last **smack** on the chin to make sure he couldn't **retaliate**. When Fanshawe looked up, holding the gun now in both hands, he saw Thomas Bates standing at the door, **glued to the spot** in shock and fear. He waved the rifle to the left, indicating to Bates that he should come in and move to the wall against which Catherine and Catesby were now leaning.

Fanshawe stepped back towards the bed and slowly shifted his **aim** from Catesby to Catherine to Bates and back again.

---

to reassure [ˌriːəˈʃɔː] beruhigen **smack** [smæk] Schlag **to retaliate** [rɪˈtælɪeɪt] zurückschlagen **to be glued to the spot** [biː ˌgluːd tə ðə ˈspɒt] wie angewurzelt sein **aim** [eɪm] Ziel

Johnson dropped his **jaw** in shock; he had seen anger on Fanshawe's face before, but never this look of possessed rage. Fanshawe's expression now was like Catesby's earlier – focussed, intense, and completely unpredictable.
"We are going to stay in this room, Robin, until you believe what Anthony has been trying to tell you. I want the three of you to listen very carefully to what I am going to say." Robin and the others looked completely bewildered. "I swear to you that what Anthony told you is true. I swear to you that we are not spies. I swear to you that we work neither for the government nor King James nor any of his agents, nor any organization that would sabotage the plot. I swear to you that from the first day we met, we have been as committed to this as you have. You have had more than a year to judge my character and Anthony's character, and we have proved ourselves to you time and time again. I need not provide examples – you know the situations that we have got ourselves into and, on occasion, you out of. We have worked together and shared your house all that time. And now you question our loyalty and our motivation because this woman whom you yourself hardly know any more overheard a few comments from outside room, late at night, and after we had all had a lot to drink? Think about it, Robin. Think about it carefully."
Johnson thought that Fanshawe sounded convincing, although in truth he hadn't provided any real evidence to support his argument. He wondered what was going through Catesby's mind. Perhaps the gun in Fanshawe's hand was the only thing about him that was convincing; perhaps it was not Fanshawe but the gun that had the at-

---

jaw [dʒɔː] Kinnlade

tention of the three people leaning against the wall. He had no way of knowing.

"Robin, I **value** your friendship as much as I believe in what we can achieve together. If you no longer want us to be part of the plot, I will be devastated, and I know I speak for both of us when I say that. If I felt that you didn't believe us, that deep down you really didn't believe us, then I would ask Anthony to join me now, and we could quite easily leave this house. But I know that you are not convinced by Catherine's story. She wants to protect you – that's perfectly natural. Perhaps she wants to scare you so that you'll abandon the plot. She's terrified of the danger involved and that you might be caught or killed. She doesn't want to lose you. So you must admit that she has a very strong reason for wanting to believe what she told you. But wanting to believe something and having evidence that it's true are two very different things, my friend. I know that deep down you find it impossible to believe her, and deep down you are right – it can't be true, because it isn't true. I'm going to prove that to you now. I'm going to prove it to you by handing you the gun. I'm handing you my trust, my sincerity, and my friendship. I'm handing you the truth. Please think carefully about what this means, Robin. If we were spies, we would simply kill you now and walk away. By handing you this gun, I am risking my life and Anthony's life. When I hand this to you, please think about the significance of that for a moment. Would a spy or an agent do such a thing?"

Fanshawe lowered the rifle and walked across the room. He slowly handed the gun to Catesby, who cautiously reached

---

to value ['vælju:] schätzen

out and took it. He looked more peaceful now, more **placid**. Johnson saw by Catesby's slow reaction that Fanshawe **had pulled off** the performance of a lifetime. If Catesby believed Fanshawe, then he must also believe that Catherine had lied, or at least wildly exaggerated. He would conclude that she had put everyone's life in danger by her foolish actions.

Even as this thought passed through his mind, Robin turned angrily on his wife and slapped her face. "You fool, Catherine. You almost made us kill each other. Do you realize what you were nearly responsible for? Have you completely lost your mind?"

Catherine continued crying as she covered her face and curled up in a bundle in the corner. Johnson's heart ached at the sight; he hated himself for what he had done and couldn't bring himself to look at Catherine. At that moment, he felt nothing but hatred for the Department and his assignment. He felt that the whole mission had been a foolish mistake, and he couldn't have cared less about its outcome. All he wanted to do was to run over to Catherine, hold her in his arms, and tell her the truth. As he lowered his head in shame and guilt, he saw the ring on his finger that Smith had given him. *Let it become a symbol of what's most important to you*, she had said, *a reminder of your real life*. As he gripped the ring and turned it round and round on his finger, he realized that his feelings for Catherine would destroy him if he didn't begin to control them. Smith was right. His real life was not here. He was searching for love in the wrong place, for the wrong reasons, at the wrong time.

---

placid ['plæsɪd] ruhig **to pull sth. off** [ˌpʊl / 'ɒf] etw. zustande bringen

Exercise 20: Put these events into *chronological* order.

a. ☐ Fanshawe returned to London.
b. ☐ Catesby woke Johnson up and threatened him.
c. ☐ Fanshawe took the rifle from Catesby.
d. ☐ Fanshawe accompanied Fawkes to the Low Countries.
e. ☐ Johnson told Catherine that Catesby wanted to kill the King.
f. ☐ Fanshawe convinced Catesby that there had been a simple misunderstanding.
g. ☐ Catesby accused Fanshawe and Johnson of spying.
h. ☐ Catherine overheard a conversation between Fanshawe and Johnson.
i. ☐ Catherine told her husband that Fanshawe and Johnson were spies.

Thirteen

Three weeks before Parliament was due to open, Johnson sat with the group at the *Duck and Drake* as they made their final preparations, ensuring that everyone knew exactly what was going to happen and what they were each responsible for. His enthusiasm for the assignment had reached a new low point and he could think of little else besides his shameful betrayal of Catherine. It took all his energy to **feign** interest in Guido's report that he and Fanshawe had successfully placed two and a half tons of gunpowder in the Whynniard cellar and hidden the thirty-six barrels beneath a small mountain of wood and coal. There was enough there, said Guido, to destroy the entire Palace of Westminster. He explained that they had spent a considerable amount of time

---

to feign [fɛɪn] vortäuschen

mixing the powder again as it **had decayed** while they were abroad, making it useless. They had had to mix each barrel again with the right amount of water and alcohol, dry it, and break it into small **crumbs**. It had been tedious and time-consuming work, he said, but now everything was in place and they were ready to carry out the assassination.

Catesby thanked Fawkes for his report and congratulated the men on stocking the cellar and **reconstituting** the powder. "Guido, when the day arrives, you will take a boat from Lambeth with Francis and Peter Fanshawe and cross the river to the Cotton Garden once more. They will wait for you in the boat while you go into the cellar and light the fuse. The three of you will then make your way down the Thames and board a merchant ship bound for the Continent. You will travel up through France and into the Low Countries to inform the exiles, Jesuit leaders, and our new allies. You must return as quickly as possible with all the men and weapons you can find."

As Catesby spoke, Percy fidgeted nervously with his glass. "My friends, I'm sorry to interrupt, but I'm afraid I have some rather disturbing news. There is to be yet another delay in the opening of Parliament. It seems the plague is still in the city, and James has now decided that Parliament won't sit until the fifth of November."

Johnson was roused from his lethargy by the men's reactions. They were **infuriated** by the news; this was now the

---

to decay [dɪˈkeɪ] *hier:* zerfallen **crumb** [krʌm] Krümel **to reconstitute** [riːˈkɒnstɪtjuːt] wiederherstellen **lethargy** [ˈleθədʒɪ] Trägheit **to be infuriated** [biː ɪnˈfjʊərɪeɪtɪd] in Wut versetzt werden

second time that the opening of Parliament had been postponed. It was originally supposed to convene on the 7th February and would not now do so until the fifth of November, a delay of nine full months.

Jack Wright stood up and began to pace around the table. "What if the plague is still around in November? Maybe it'll be delayed again until next year? Is James using the plague as an excuse to hide some other reason for not wanting Parliament to sit? Perhaps he has been warned of our plot? Is that it?"

Catesby sat back in his chair, his **countenance** grim in the face of the disappointing news. "All right, all right, come on – sit down, Jack, I know this is frustrating but let's not jump to any conclusions. There's nothing we can do about it – it's beyond our control. At least it's only a month this time. Look – everything is in place. You should all go back to your normal routines and avoid contact with each other from now on. We need to make sure that we don't give anyone a reason to suspect anything. This delay may in fact work to our advantage. I'll go north again to inform our friends and perhaps raise some more support. Anthony, perhaps you could join me on this trip?"

Catesby's request took Johnson by surprise. He had known, of course, that the opening of Parliament would be delayed again, and hadn't been paying a great deal of attention to the conversation. With the tension between himself and Catherine now unbearable, he had reluctantly begun to accept that there could be no reconciliation between them. Sleeping under the same roof as Catherine now would only **exacerbate**

---

countenance ['kaʊntənəns] Antlitz **to exacerbate** [ɪg'zæsəbeɪt] verschlimmern

the pain that both of them were in. As much as he wanted to tell her the truth and live out the rest of his life with her here, he knew that this would not happen. He would reluctantly see out the rest of the assignment and return to his life at the university in Oxford. For now, he felt the right thing to do would be to get away from Catherine for a while. He took a deep breath and looked up at Catesby.

"Yes, Robin, I'd be happy to join you."

Johnson knew that by joining Catesby on his trip he would be away from London until the end of October, and would most likely miss out on the opportunity to observe many of the events that the Department wanted **clarified**. By now, however, his enthusiasm for the mission had worn thin and he cared little about uncovering the details of the plot; he could think only of Catherine and of the pain he had caused her. For the first time in his life he had felt that it might have been possible to overcome his fear of loss and to give himself completely to someone else. Catherine had brought out the best in him; she had made him feel happy about who he was and given him the confidence to be himself without having to worry that he would be judged for his actions or opinions. But he had thrown it all away; he had convinced himself that it would all have to end when he returned to the future, and that it would be less painful for Catherine if they separated earlier rather than later. Perhaps he could have told her the truth – about time travel and how he came to be there, and about his real life. Perhaps she would have believed him.

Catesby told the men that they would all meet for the last time on the first of November. He paused briefly, then

---

clarified ['klærəfaɪd] geklärt

gently whispered, "And finally, gentlemen, I know that some of you have suffered doubts and struggled with the moral justification of what we are about to do. I remind you once again of what St Thomas Aquinas himself **preached** almost four hundred years ago: it is morally defensible to overthrow a tyrant as long as the affected population suffer less as a result of the rebellion than they did before. Now more than ever we can have no doubt in our hearts about what we are about to undertake. Nevertheless, it is natural that you will all have some remaining worries. I would encourage you all to confess your sins to the Lord in order to give you the strength you will need in the coming weeks. Father Tesimond is waiting in the room next door."

Although Johnson was not a Catholic, he welcomed this opportunity to relieve the **burden** of guilt that he carried in his heart. Under the **seal of the confessional**, Johnson could speak freely in the knowledge that the priest could not **divulge** what he had heard to another living soul; he could not even use this information to save the lives of innocent people. For months Johnson had desperately wanted to talk to someone openly. He could speak with Fanshawe about their real lives and the burden of living in the past with all of its restrictions and responsibilities; but there was no one he could confide in about the one thing that mattered to him more than any other – his feelings for Catherine. It would be another four and a half months before he could return to his normal life and put this epi-

---

to preach [priːtʃ] predigen **burden** [ˈbɜːdn] Last **seal of the confessional** [ˌsiːl əv ðə kənˈfeʃnəl] Beichtgeheimnis **to divulge** [daɪˈvʌldʒ] preisgeben

sode behind him. He hoped that the distance from Catherine would help him to overcome his pain and depression; he prayed that returning to the familiar surroundings of Oxford in 2055 would allow him to heal. If only there were some magic pill he could swallow, some secret button he could press that would transport him back to his real life this instant, he would have gone **without hesitation**, but neither he nor Fanshawe could control when they would return. He would have to wait until the appointed time.

Exercise 21: Which words are opposites?

1. to welcome	☐	**a.** to bring forward	
2. to be guilty	☐	**b.** to lose	
3. to whisper	☐	**c.** to succumb to	
4. to overcome	☐	**d.** to be innocent	
5. to delay	☐	**e.** to be certain	
6. to gain	☐	**f.** to shout	
7. to doubt	☐	**g.** to dread	

As the men stood up and went to confess their sins to the Jesuit priest one after another, Catesby moved down the length of the table to sit beside Johnson, putting a friendly hand on the professor's shoulder. "Don't look so grim, Anthony. It's only another seven weeks."

As Johnson looked up quickly at Catesby's sympathetic smile, it took him a moment to realize that Robin must have noticed his despondency and assumed that it was caused by the delay in the opening of Parliament. "Yes, yes, of course."

---

without hesitation [wɪðˌaʊt hezɪ'teɪʃn] ohne zu zögern

"Tell me, then, what dark secrets will you be revealing to Father Tesimond?"
If only you knew, he thought, as he smiled back at Catesby. "Oh, nothing he hasn't heard before, I expect, Robin, you know, all the usual stuff – greed, lust, **gluttony**, **sloth**, envy, wrath, pride – that kind of thing."
"It sounds like he may have to work overtime tonight."
"Well I certainly hope he hasn't made any dinner arrangements."
Out of the corner of his eye, Johnson spotted Fanshawe getting up at the other end of the table and leaving through the back door to visit the priest. Johnson was suddenly gripped with an irrational curiosity about what Fanshawe would say to Father Tesimond. With the freedom of the seal of the confessional, Fanshawe too might wish to unburden himself of his private thoughts. It occurred to Johnson that he and Fanshawe had not had an intimate conversation in months. While they hadn't argued since the day they had witnessed the execution, neither had their conversations extended beyond superficial discussions about the plot. He realized now that he had no idea what was going on in his companion's mind. He wondered now for the first time whether Fanshawe suspected anything about his feelings for Catherine. Was it possible that Fanshawe was more sensitive and discreet than Johnson had given him credit for? Perhaps Fanshawe did know but chose to feign ignorance, knowing that Johnson would be suffering terribly. Johnson was slightly disturbed by the look on Fanshawe's face when he returned a few minutes later and sat at the table in silence, slowly sipping his beer and staring at

---

gluttony ['glʌtnɪ] Gefräßigkeit **sloth** [sləʊθ] Faulheit

the candle in the centre of the table. He appeared to be deep in thought, as if intensely focussed on something that had happened during his confession. Johnson had seen this expression once before – when Fanshawe had overpowered Catesby and taken the rifle from him. What words could have passed between Fanshawe and the priest? What thoughts could have led to such uncharacteristic intensity? He wondered if Fanshawe could possibly still be thinking about making sure that the plot succeeded. He had clearly grown to respect Guido on their trip abroad, and his sensitive and affectionate nature would surely have some influence on his feelings for the men. His knowledge of their certain death must be playing heavily on his mind; but what could Johnson do? What right did he now have to persuade Fanshawe of the importance of leaving history alone? By telling Catherine about the plot, Johnson knew that he had put the mission at great risk. Wouldn't it sound **hypocritical** to try to persuade Fanshawe not to interfere?

As Johnson got up from the table and walked towards the back door of the *Duck and Drake*, Fanshawe's gaze remained fixed on the candle. He didn't react when Johnson put a friendly hand on his shoulder as he passed him on his way out. When the professor entered the room that he and Fanshawe had stood outside the night they arrived, he saw Father Tesimond sitting in a darkened corner of the bare room, his elbows resting on his knees, and his head buried in his hands. As Johnson approached him and knelt down on the stone floor, the priest rubbed his eyes and slowly sat up; he looked exhausted, as if carrying an enormous burden from what he had heard over the past half an hour.

---

hypocritical [ˌhɪpəˈkrɪtɪkl] heuchlerisch

Whatever Fanshawe had said to the priest, Johnson knew that his own confession would be markedly different from those of the other men; he almost felt pleased that he might be giving Father Tesimond some **respite** from the shocking confessions he would have listened to up to now.

"Father, forgive me. I have betrayed my friend. I have betrayed the woman I love, and I have betrayed myself."

The priest, dressed in **layman's clothe**s for protection, paused to consider what Johnson had said. "Jesus said, 'What you do to the least of my **brethren**, you do to me.' Betrayal is very serious, my son. When you betray those around you, you are betraying God. It was betrayal that led to the crucifixion of Christ himself. What form has this betrayal taken?"

"Lies, deception, half-truths, **misrepresentation** of reality, hiding my true identity from myself and others, **distorting** facts to suit my needs."

"If you wish to ask for the Lord's forgiveness, you must feel true remorse at your actions. You must be sincere in your commitment to change your behaviour, and you must speak the truth to those around you from this point forward. Can you make this commitment before God?"

Johnson gave a deep sigh and lowered his head to his hands in shame. He had hoped that the confession would have a **cathartic** effect, but now that he was here he couldn't bring himself to speak freely; he didn't have the courage to articulate his sins beyond these generalities, and in his heart

---

respite ['respaɪt] *hier*: Abwechslung **laymen's clothes** ['leɪmənz ˌkləʊðz] normale Kleidung **brethren** ['breðrən] Brüder **misrepresentation** [ˌmɪsreprɪzen'teɪʃn] falsche Darstellung **to distort** [dɪ'stɔːt] verzerren **cathartic** [kə'θɑːtɪk] reinigend

he knew that he could not do what the priest was asking of him.
"No, Father, I don't think I can."

Fourteen

Catesby was feeling irritated. It was the day that he was due to ride north with Johnson, and he was searching **in vain** for his riding boots in the bedroom where he slept on the increasingly rare occasions when he stayed at home. His wife had had her own room at the other end of the corridor for more than a year now, an arrangement that caused him little worry or concern. They had adopted a polite and functional tone in their conversations, speaking only when necessary, and never out of a need for companionship. Not a word had passed between them since the fiasco that had almost made him kill the two men.
As the sun rose and he looked under the bed for a third time, he noticed a pair of feet on the other side of the room. He peered over the bed to see Catherine leaning against the doorframe, staring impassively at her husband and drinking a large glass of wine, despite the early hour.
"Catherine, have you seen my riding boots? I've looked everywhere and I can't find the damn things."
"I'm leaving you, Robin."
Robin turned and slowly rose to his feet as a look of bitterness and anger came across his face. "You're drunk."
"I'm taking Robert with me and moving in with my parents. We won't be here when you get back."

---

in vain [ɪn 'veɪn] vergebens

"Is this about the plot?"
"No, Robin, it's about the fact that I hate you. I hate the sight of you. I hate the thought of you. I hate the sound of your voice. I hate the way you smell. And I hate you for making your son grow up with the knowledge that his father was a mass murderer."
"So it *is* about the plot." Robin forced a look of irritation, returning to his search for the boots in order to deny the importance of the conversation and suggest that Catherine was being over-dramatic.

Exercise 22: Robin can't see what's happening in front of his eyes, but for Catherine everything is as easy as ABC.
Fill in the following words correctly.
(attention, blind, consumed, door, even, face, guilty, having, idiocy)

"You're so **1.** ______________, Robin. You're so **2.** ______________ with yourself that you don't even see what's going on around you. You're like a little boy crying out for **3.** ______________, and you don't realize that you only get it to keep you quiet."
"And what of it? I'd rather be **4.** ______________ of being an attention-seeker than of **5.** ______________ lost all touch with reality. And it might just be possible, Catherine, that I'm a bit more **observant** than you think."

---

observant [əb'zɜːvənt] aufmerksam

"Ha! That's good, coming from a man who can't **6.** ____________ find his own shoes!" Catherine bent down and picked his boots up from under a chair by the **7.** ____________. She held them up for Robin to see, a look of **smug** satisfaction on her **8.** ____________ as she **paraded** the evidence of his **9.** ____________ before him. "Tell me then, if you're so observant, what you know about my affair with Anthony?"

Robin gave a brief, condescending laugh, intended to suggest that Catherine was simply lying in order to irritate and provoke him further.

"Oh, so you didn't notice that your new best friend was sleeping with your wife? How very observant of you, Robin. You never thought about what we used to do on our long daily walks together? What did you think? That we were getting some fresh air and picking flowers?"
"You're out of your mind, Catherine. I know what you're trying to do, and it won't work."
"Fine. Don't take my word for it. Ask Anthony, he'll tell you, if he has any **decency** left. Telling you the truth about what happened between us is the least he can do before he sends you to the gallows. I hope you kill each other. I hope you strangle each other and die in the dirt before you kill all

---

smug [smʌg] selbstgefällig **to parade** [pəˈreɪd] vorführen **decency** [ˈdiːsnsɪ] Anstand

those innocent people." Catherine threw her empty glass at Robin who had to duck behind the bed to avoid being hit. The glass smashed against the wall as Catherine ran back to her own room and slammed the door.

Robin finished packing and pulled on his riding boots. When he arrived downstairs he found Johnson waiting for him in the living room. "Ready?" he asked, forcing a cheerful smile. They mounted their horses and rode out through the early morning fog. Catesby made a point of staying slightly ahead of Johnson for the first few hours, not wanting to invite a conversation by riding parallel. They stopped to eat in the early afternoon halfway between London and Oxford at the hamlet of Reading, a small cluster of dusty shacks hugging both banks of the River Thames, with a single dark and filthy tavern called the Oracle. Once they were seated and had ordered two plates of lamb and two ales, Catesby looked at Johnson nervously. "I think Catherine's imagination is running away with her again."

"Is that so?"

"You won't believe what she told me this morning." Catesby knew he was taking a risk in confronting Johnson with this; he had no idea whether Catherine had completely lost touch with reality or not, and after the debacle about whether or not Johnson and Fanshawe were spies, he knew he couldn't take anything she said at face value. Although she had been drunk and angry when she confronted him this morning, she had also been utterly convincing in what she had told him. The question that tormented Catesby now wasn't whether or not Catherine had been sincere – it was clear that she had been – but whether or not she had lost all touch with reality and had imagined the things that she had said to him. He needed to get it off his chest and be done with it.

"She claims that the two of you had some kind of **clandestine** affair." Although he said it with sarcasm to emphasize how ridiculous the suggestion was, he found himself anxiously praying that Johnson would deny it. In truth, he was more afraid that Johnson might have kept a secret from him than the thought that his wife had betrayed him. His heart sank as Johnson lowered his head and stared down at the table.

"I'm sorry, Robin."

Catesby didn't respond. What need was there now to speak more of this? He felt his eyes becoming heavy and swollen as Johnson raised his head to speak.

"I … It was … I had …"

He looked as if he were in great pain, but Robin didn't care to know whether it was because of his betrayal or his love for Catherine.

Johnson looked at him again. "Don't you care?"

He couldn't look at Johnson; he shifted his gaze to the other customers in the tavern, pretending that the news had had little effect on him.

"The only thing I care about now is making sure that James dies."

Fifteen

Fanshawe began to follow Tresham on the day of his father's funeral in mid-September. Keeping out of sight behind a large oak tree in a distant corner of the cemetery, he

---

clandestine [klæn'destɪn] heimlich

saw Tresham with his seven brothers and sisters and their **grieving** mother standing over the grave as a priest in layman's clothes quietly prayed for the departed soul of Sir Thomas Tresham. Fanshawe noticed a cold and distant look in Tresham's eyes, as if he were not only unaffected by his father's death, but as if his mind were entirely occupied by other thoughts. No sooner had his father's **corpse** been buried than Francis made to move, visibly eager to get away from the graveyard.

Within two days of the funeral, Tresham had resumed his usual daily routine, and went about his business with an air of gravity that might be expected from a man who had just lost a close relative. Fanshawe wondered whether his **gloomy** countenance resulted from the pain of his loss or the torment of his thoughts about betraying the plot. Tresham rose each morning shortly after dawn and took breakfast in the front room of the house with his wife, Anne, and their two young daughters, Lucy and Eliza. As Anne prepared the girls for their private lessons, Fanshawe looked on from across the street, hidden from view by the shadows in the alley where he stood. Every day he watched as Tresham left the house and went for a long walk through the streets of Hoxton and Shoreditch, consistently following the same route. His journey always ended at a small, oval church with stained-glass windows that threw watery **turquoise** light on the wooden **pews** within. Here, amid the statues and the silence, only God and Fanshawe knew that Tresham's prayers were those of a Catholic, and only

---

grieving ['gri:vɪŋ] trauernd **corpse** [kɔ:ps] Leiche **gloomy** ['glu:mɪ] düster **turquoise** ['tɜ:kwɔɪz] türkis **pew** [pju:] Kirchenbank

God and Fanshawe could guess at the substance of his thoughts.

Fanshawe spent six weeks hiding in doorways and back streets, **lurking** outside Tresham's home and following him on his daily walks. On the third morning, Tresham turned around unexpectedly, scanning the street behind him and causing Fanshawe's heart to race. At that moment, Fanshawe knew he couldn't maintain a safe distance and still keep a watchful eye on Tresham; he had to change his appearance in order to get closer. It occurred to him that the rich tended to avoid the gaze of the poor; if their eyes met, a human bond was formed, however brief, that gave birth to expectation and discomfort **in equal measure**. He bought ochre and red sandalwood to **dye** his hair and beard; he worked mud into his clothes, his shoes and his face, and he began to affect a slight **limp**, making it impossible to distinguish him from all the other beggars who **criss-crossed** the city from break of day until darkness descended. Fanshawe now took to the streets with renewed determination, his confidence **buoyed up** by yet another new identity. As he became convinced of his ability to keep his true identity hidden, the playful side of his nature returned, the same **mischievous** trait that had almost exposed him and Johnson on the night they had arrived back in the past. On days when the complete lack of variety in Tresham's routine caused Fanshawe to become **numb** with

---

to lurk [lɜːk] lauern **in equal measure** [ɪn ˌiːkwəl ˈmeʒə] gleichermaßen **to dye** [daɪ] färben **limp** [lɪmp] Hinken **to criss-cross** [ˈkrɪskrɒs] kreuz und quer laufen **to be buoyed up** [biː ˌbɔɪd ˈʌp] gestärkt werden **mischievous** [ˈmɪstʃɪvəs] schelmisch **numb** [nʌm] betäubt

boredom, he would amuse himself by seeing how close he could get to Tresham without being noticed. On several occasions he walked directly behind him, sometimes even overtaking him and leading the way to the small oval church. He was often tempted to approach Tresham and beg for money, but fortunately he still exhibited a healthy degree of both reason and cowardice.

Exercise 23: Fanshawe is getting bored observing Tresham. He amuses himself by creating anagrams of concepts associated with the Gunpowder Plot. Can you solve the anagrams and match each one up correctly?

1. an explosive substance	☐	**a.** rabler
2. a place first flooded, then abandoned	☐	**b.** tertel
3. a persecuted minority	☐	**c.** pedwourng
4. a container for gunpowder	☐	**d.** nelnut
5. Monteagle found out about the plot by a ...	☐	**e.** sicchatol

On October 26th, Fanshawe left the Catesby house while it was still dark outside. When he was halfway to Tresham's home, he slipped into a damp alleyway between two large buildings. Carefully avoiding the giant rats that **zigzagged** back and forth in a frantic search for something edible, he took out his beggar's outfit and picked up some mud from the street to rub into his face and hair. He then removed a pile of bricks from the back of the alley and collected the gun that he had hidden there a week earlier, carefully wrapped in a foul-smelling cloth to

---

to zigzag ['zɪgzæg] sich im Zickzack bewegen

repel the curiosity of anyone who might chance upon it. When he reached Tresham's home, he moved to the alley on the opposite side of the road from the house and waited for an hour. The time when Tresham normally emerged from the house came and went, and Fanshawe could see no movement through the windows to suggest that he was merely slightly delayed today. When another hour had passed, he began to panic. *What if Tresham wasn't even at home? What if he had left in the middle of the night? Where was he? Had these six weeks been a complete waste of time?* Another hour passed as Fanshawe paced up and down the street, constantly shifting his eyes from one window to the next in a desperate search for signs of life within. It took him almost two hours to remember that it was Saturday and that the Tresham family always rose a little later at the weekend. Finally, at nine o'clock, he saw Anne standing at an upstairs window, **tying** her hair back with both hands, and glimpsed Tresham in the room behind her.

As he stood waiting for Francis to appear at the front door, an oppressive blanket of thick dark clouds moved across the sky, blocking out the last remnants of natural daylight. The only respite from the darkness came in momentary flashes of lightning, followed by the rumble and boom of thunder that got louder and closer by the minute. As a light **drizzle** turned quickly into a **torrential downpour**, Fanshawe tried to imagine the scene inside the house – Tresham sitting down to breakfast with his wife and children, laughing and joking in the warmth of the family home,

---

to repel [rɪ'pel] abwehren **to tie** [taɪ] binden **drizzle** ['drɪzl] Nieselregen **torrential** [tə'renʃl] sintflutartig **downpour** ['daʊnpɔː] Platzregen

when all the while he was perhaps planning to betray his friends, his relatives, and the entire Catholic population of the country. How could he believe that what he was doing was right? How could he betray the love and loyalty of Robin, Percy and the others, knowing that by saving the lives of the King and his parliamentarians, he would be condemning the others to death, and English Catholics to further persecution? Fanshawe kept his head lowered and pulled the large hood down as far as possible to prevent the rain from washing the mud from his face. Now **soaked to the skin** and shivering with the cold, he stood at the corner for another six hours, desperately wondering why Tresham had not yet left the house. Was it because of the significance of the date? Was he expecting someone to visit him at home? Monteagle, perhaps? If Tresham didn't leave the house today, would that mean that somebody else was responsible for informing Monteagle? Was it possible that Tresham was just history's **scapegoat**, an innocent framed by historians in the absence of conclusive evidence? At three o'clock in the afternoon, as Fanshawe went over the possibilities again and again in his mind, and with the rain still pouring down, Tresham finally emerged from the house. Fanshawe felt weak with relief and had to lean against the wall to steady himself. As he regained his **composure**, he saw Tresham take one brief look up and down the street before walking briskly in his usual direction. He moved at his normal pace and made no attempt to avoid the large **puddles** that had gathered at every corner.

---

soaked to the skin [ˌsəʊkt tə ðə ˈskɪn] tropfnass **scapegoat** [ˈskeɪpgəʊt] Sündenbock **composure** [kəmˈpəʊʒə] Fassung **puddle** [ˈpʌdl] Pfütze

As Fanshawe walked the familiar route through the city for the thirty-fifth time, he had to keep a greater distance than usual between himself and Tresham; the heavy rain had forced people to stay indoors and there was no crowd for Fanshawe to blend into. Although he stayed more than two hundred metres behind Tresham, there wasn't a single person between them for the duration of their walk. On several occasions he dropped back so far that he lost sight of the man, but the route made him confident that Tresham's destination was again the oval church. When Fanshawe came within a few hundred metres of the church, he crossed the street and quickened his pace to make sure that Tresham did indeed go in. He moved into the shadows in his usual doorway just in time to see Tresham pull back the heavy wooden door of the church and slip quietly inside.

Before the door had closed fully behind him, Fanshawe stepped out onto the road. He looked left and right, an instinctive habit learned in childhood that he hadn't managed to shake off here, even though he was unlikely to be hit by any speeding traffic. He moved quickly across the street and around to the side of the church. Pressing his face up against the stained-glass window, he saw a shadow moving slowly up the central **aisle**. The dark silhouette **genuflected** in front of the altar and then knelt down in the front pew. Fanshawe ran back to the entrance of the church and pulled the door open. He took up his normal position in the pew right at the back, from where he could see Tresham kneeling and staring straight ahead at the statue of Christ raised high at the back of the altar. Tresham prayed for almost thirty minutes, twice the amount of

---

aisle [aɪl] Gang **to genuflect** ['dʒenjʊflekt] das Knie beugen

time that he would normally spend in the church before returning home. He rose from his knees, genuflected once more before the altar, and made the sign of the cross, touching his right hand against his head, chest and shoulders. As he walked back down the aisle, Fanshawe pulled his large hood over his head, making sure his face was hidden from view as Tresham passed him and left the church.

As soon as he heard the door close, Fanshawe got up from his knees and ran outside. As he instinctively turned his head to the left, he found himself hoping that he wouldn't see Tresham walking in the direction that he would normally take to return home. He had invested so much time and energy over the past month and a half **concocting** an image in his mind of Tresham as the Judas Iscariot of the plotters that he would actually have been terribly disappointed to discover otherwise. Not seeing Tresham on either side of the street, Fanshawe held his breath as he turned to look in the opposite direction. He scanned the street up and down, frantically looking through the thick crowds of people for a glimpse of Tresham, and there, about a hundred metres from the church, he saw him looking back towards it as he crossed the road. Fanshawe hurried down the steps in front of the church and kept his head lowered as he followed Tresham through the city. From the route they were taking, Fanshawe knew within minutes that Tresham was now moving in the direction of Lord Monteagle's house, hurrying through the streets completely unaware that he was being followed by a man determined to prevent him from carrying out his mission.

---

to concoct [kən'kɒkt] zusammenbasteln

Exercise 24: Put in the right proposition to make a suitable phrasal verb.
(down, out, over, up (2x), off, in)

1. Johnson tried to win ________ the students.
2. Johnson carried ________ a masterful performance.
3. Johnson couldn't take ________ the implications of what he had seen.
4. Fanshawe set ________ to achieve a miracle.
5. Johnson and Fanshawe settled ________ in seventeenth-century London.
6. Johnson had to make ________ some details of his biography.
7. Fanshawe took ________ his usual position in the church.

Sixteen

Catherine remained true to her word and moved out of the house the day that Catesby and Johnson rode north. She took her son and a few belongings and moved in with her parents, but she had neither the courage nor the **inclination** to explain the full story to them. She simply told them that her relationship with Robin **had deteriorated** over the

---

inclination [ˌɪnklɪˈneɪʃn] Lust **to deteriorate** [dɪˈtɪərɪəreɪt] sich verschlechtern

past several months and that she needed to get away to be alone with her thoughts. The little that she told them was the truth, if only a small part of the story. Her only lie was to say that the separation would be a temporary arrangement; she knew that she would never again sleep under the same roof as her husband. Catherine felt ill at the thought of returning to her own house to collect the rest of her belongings, but she was expecting the men to return to London in the last days of October, so she decided to get this unpleasant task over with on Saturday, the twenty-sixth. She had arranged for a transport-carriage to arrive later in the day when she had gone through everything, preferring to be left alone to **tag** the items to be removed. As she walked up the stairs and into the bedroom that she and her husband had once shared, she was overcome by a terrible sense of loss, a grief she hadn't felt since her first child had died years before. She had now lost everyone she loved, with the exception of her second son. It made her deeply unhappy having to move back in with her parents; she despised her father and tolerated her mother but she had nowhere else to go and so had little choice. As the days and weeks had passed, she had found herself feeling as alone in her parents' house as she had in her own.

Catherine sat down at the cherry-wood **dressing table** by the window that looked out over the grounds at the front of the house. She picked up a few small **trinkets**, mostly earrings and necklaces she had received as gifts from Robin in the early years of their marriage. Staring at them now in her hand they looked unfamiliar, as if she were seeing them

---

to tag [tæg] etikettieren **dressing table** ['dresɪŋ ˌteɪbl] Frisierkommode **trinket** ['trɪŋkɪt] billiges Schmuckstück

for the first time, as though they belonged to someone else. What were they worth to her now? What value was to be found in such tokens of love when the love had long since died? She placed them back on the table and stared at the reflection in the oval mirror. She barely recognized the face that looked back at her; the woman she saw looked **withered** and tired, as if she had already come to the end of her life and was ready for eternal rest. Although it was the men in her life who had consistently let her down, she suffered from attacks of anxiety and intense feelings of guilt and worthlessness, as though she alone were responsible for her failed relationships. Her guilt was compounded by constant exhaustion; she couldn't understand why she felt so lethargic all the time. She was sleeping for twelve or fourteen hours every day and no longer had the energy or the desire to go for the walks that had once given her such pleasure.

Finally she moved to the wardrobe and took out the few items of clothing that held no strong memories for her, the neutral pieces that she had bought when she was alone, ones that Robin had never commented on. As she knelt down to pick up her shoes from the bottom of the wardrobe, she noticed a small box at the back. She removed the lid and took out a small, heavy **parcel**. Inside a thick piece of linen, she found a pistol. It was clear that Robin was taking no chances; if his plot was discovered he would not be taken from his house without a struggle.

How had things come to this, she wondered? How could her husband's world be so different from her own? Was he always this person, or had he turned into such a dangerous

---

withered ['wɪðəd] hutzelig **parcel** ['pɑːsl] Päckchen

and unpleasant character during their **estrangement**? Had she ever really known him? Had there ever been any meaning or worth to their marriage? She remembered his time in prison, of course, and for as long as she had known him he had always talked about the plight of the Catholics, but his actions now took things to a new level. What was it, she asked herself, that had turned him from a mere angry citizen into a man **bent on wreaking** such havoc? Holding the gun in her hand, she walked a few paces to the edge of the bed and sat down. All around her were symbols of loss and death; all around her were reminders of her failed life. She now had both the motivation and the means to put an end to her suffering.

As her tears fell onto the cold steel in her hands, Catherine heard the sound of horses galloping towards the house. She went to the window and saw Robin and Anthony approaching fast. She began to panic. What were they doing back so early? They weren't supposed to arrive home for at least another three or four days. She dreaded the prospect of meeting them; these were the last two people on earth she wished to see.

Realizing that her coat was hanging in the hall, she threw the box back into the wardrobe and ran downstairs, wiping away her tears with one hand while still holding the gun in the other. As the men **dismounted** and lifted their bags off the horses, she grabbed her coat and ran into the living room, not knowing where she was going or what she was going to do. Hearing the sound of footsteps getting closer

---

estrangement [ɪ'streɪndʒmənt] Entfremdung **to be bent on doing sth.** [biː ˌbent ɒn 'duːɪŋ] darauf versessen sein, etw. zu tun
to wreak [riːk] anrichten **to dismount** [dɪs'maʊnt] absteigen

to the front door, she put her coat on and slipped behind one of the heavy curtains that stretched from floor to ceiling. She could now hear her heart beating and the sound of her own breathing as the men entered the house. She was terrified at the thought of them finding her, and yet her own fear confused her. Why did she feel so sick at the thought of seeing them? Of course it would be briefly awkward and unpleasant, but wasn't she overreacting? She wasn't a **burglar**, after all; this was her own home and she had merely come to claim what was hers. A strong woman would have confronted the men, she thought. A strong woman would have made a point of taking her things and walking straight past them and out of the house with her head held high. If the men found her hiding behind the curtain she would look ridiculous; she would look as weak and foolish as she now felt. It would confirm Robin's theory that she had indeed gone mad. The more she thought about her own behaviour, the more she hated herself.

Exercise 25: "The more she thought about her own behaviour, the more she hated herself." Put in the correct comparative form of each adjective.

1. The *(far)* ____________ you travel back in time, the *(tricky)* ____________ it is to adapt to the local conditions.
2. The *(long)* ____________ Fanshawe stayed in the seventeenth century, the *(sympathetic)* ____________ he felt towards the plotters.

---

burglar ['bɜːglə] Einbrecherin

3. The *(close)* ________________ her husband and Johnson came to the curtain, the *(uncomfortable)* ________________ Catherine felt.

4. Johnson said, "The *(intelligent)* ________________ the pupil, the *(good)* ______________."

5. The *(loud)* ________________ Catherine shouted at Johnson, the *(bad)* ____________ he felt.

As she stood as quietly as possible with her hands and face brushing against the rough fabric of the curtain, she heard Robin and Anthony speaking as they moved down the hall, **presumably** on their way to the back kitchen to hang up their wet cloaks. She inhaled the dust in her **confined** space, desperately trying not to sneeze, while **retracing** in her mind the movements she had made about the house. She made a mental list of the rooms she had been in and whether she might have left any evidence of her presence. She was wearing her coat, she had replaced the box in the wardrobe, and her horse was **tethered** out of sight at the back of the house. She couldn't think of any reason why they should suspect anything. As she went over her movements a second time, she heard Robin and Anthony come into the living room. She held her breath as they moved slowly towards the two couches that faced each other by the fireplace. It was clear from the sound of their voices

---

presumably [prɪ'zjuːməblɪ] vermutlich **confined** [kən'faɪnd] beengt **to retrace** [rɪ'treɪs] zurückgehen **to be tethered** [biː 'teðəd] angebunden sein

that Robin was putting wooden logs together to warm up the room as Anthony stood at the drinks cabinet filling glasses. It took all her strength and concentration to remain still as she listened to her husband speak.

"She's obviously more stubborn than I thought."

"What do you mean?"

"Catherine. She said she was moving out and taking Robert with her. I didn't believe her. I thought she was just drunk and in one of her childish moods."

"Where would she have gone?"

"To her parents. She has nowhere else to go. Although if she found me hard to deal with, God knows how she can put up with that father of hers. She'll come crawling back before long."

"I thought you didn't care any more?"

"I do care about seeing my son, Anthony."

Catherine was surprised to find that she felt no emotion at hearing Robin speak like that. She was even curious to hear more of her husband's cold-hearted opinions, but the silence that fell upon the room betrayed the uneasiness that this topic had created between the men, and just as she expected, Robin soon changed the subject.

"So what will you do now in the coming days?"

"I'm going to contact Guido tomorrow and get him to take me to the cellar. I want to see it with my own eyes before it's reduced to **rubble**."

"Be careful, Anthony, we don't want to raise too many suspicions, especially now, when we are so close to the big day."

"Don't worry, we'll be discreet."

---

rubble [ˈrʌbl] Trümmer

"Well, for now I'm going to worry about getting some rest. I'm exhausted. I'll see you sometime this evening, I expect."

"Yes, sleep well. I'll go up for some rest soon myself."

Catherine listened as her husband rose from the couch and left the room. As Robin walked slowly up the stairs, she heard Anthony pick up his glass and shuffle around the room. Her heart began to quicken when she realized that he was walking towards her. Despite the cold, beads of sweat started to form on her forehead and her knees went weak with fear. He was only inches away from her now; he was so close to her that if he had put his hand on his hip, he would have hit her with his elbow. The sound of him breathing beside her brought back bittersweet memories of their intimate moments together. It also reminded her of his cruel betrayal and his murderous lies. As she struggled to remain calm she heard Robin's bedroom door closing. The curtain flapped against her as Anthony moved quickly away from the window. She heard him put his glass on the table and hurry out of the room down the hallway. She waited quietly until she heard the front door being gently closed. Looking out of the window behind her, she saw Anthony pull his cloak on as he mounted his horse. Without thinking, Catherine ran to the back door of the house and jumped on her own horse. She realized that Robin would hear the sound of two horses a few minutes apart and come to the window. She no longer cared if he saw her racing away from the house. She galloped after Anthony in the pouring rain, not knowing why, and not sure what she would do if she caught up with him.

Seventeen

Johnson's enthusiasm for the assignment had not entirely returned, but having arrived back a few days early on this significant date, he knew he would have been a fool not to take the opportunity to join Fanshawe in finding out the truth about Tresham and the Monteagle letter. It was just past three o'clock in the afternoon when Robin retired and Johnson climbed back on his horse; he was anxious that he might already be too late to observe the day's crucial developments by the time he arrived at Monteagle's house.

He pushed his horse as fast as she would go through the pouring rain, although the poor beast was exhausted from the long journey and could manage little more than a canter. As he **goaded** her gently, patting her neck and speaking soft words of apology and encouragement, he thought of each of the plotters and of how close they all were to disaster. He wondered what each of them was doing on this Saturday afternoon, unaware that they were being betrayed by one of their friends and that, ten days from now, **their fates would be sealed.**

He thought of Guido, captured in the cellar the night before parliament was due to open, then placed in handcuffs and stretched on the **rack** under King James's personal instructions. He thought of Guido's courage, holding out under torture for days in the hope that his friends would have enough time to flee. As the centuries passed, of course, Guido would become the symbol of the whole enterprise, the only member of the group whose name

---

to goad [gəʊd] antreiben **their fates would be sealed** [ðeə 'feɪts wʊd bɪ 'siːld] ihr Schicksal wäre besiegelt **rack** [ræk] Streckbank

would be remembered. He would soon become a figure of hatred and **revulsion**, the so-called '**Devil of the Vault**'.

As his mare regained a measure of energy and picked up her **pace**, Johnson thought of the fate that **lay in store** for the other men. He thought of how Guido's resilience would indeed give the others time to ride north, reaching Staffordshire before a local sheriff and a band of two hundred **vigilantes** caught up with them at the home of a sympathizer. Catesby and Percy would be killed by a single bullet, minutes after watching the Wright brothers and John Grant being shot. The others would be captured, tried, and sentenced; the Wintours, Thomas Bates, Robert Keyes, Ambrose Rookwood and Sir Everard Digby would be hung, drawn, and quartered before an outraged and bloodthirsty public. By a strange twist of fate, only Francis Tresham would die of natural causes, succumbing to a **urinary tract infection** while still a prisoner in the Tower.

As Johnson entered a wood not far from Monteagle's house, he saw two dark figures in the distance standing several feet apart. The wind and heavy rain prevented him from recognizing them until he was almost upon them. As he approached, he wiped the rain from his face and threw back the hood of his cloak. What he saw caused him anguish and confusion in equal measure. There stood Fanshawe, his arm outstretched, tightly clutching a gun which he was pointing directly at Tresham.

---

revulsion [rɪˈvʌlʃn] Abscheu **Devil of the Vault** [ˌdevl əv ðə ˈvɔːlt] *Derjenige, der gemeint ist, wenn man „vom Teufel spricht."* **pace** [peɪs] Tempo **to lie (lay, lain) in store** [ˌlaɪ / leɪ / leɪn ɪn ˈstɔː] bevorstehen **vigilante** [ˌvɪdʒɪˈlæntɪ] Mitglied einer Bürgerwehr **urinary tract infection** [ˈjʊərɪnərɪ trækt ɪnˌfekʃn] Infektion der Harnwege

Exercise 26: Fill in the verbs and make sure that they are in the right tense.

Johnson **1.** *(to shout)* ______________ from his horse while still galloping towards the men. "Peter, what in God's name **2.** *(to do)* __________ you __________?"

"I won't let him do it. *I won't let him do it!*"

"**3.** *(to lose)* _________ you ____________ your mind? After everything we **4.** *(to be)* __________ through? After everything we've talked about? Have you forgotten the Sacred Rule?"

For the third time, Johnson **5.** *(to see)* ____________ that **crazed**, possessed look in Fanshawe's eyes. "You **6.** *(to be)* ____________ right, Johnson. There is no letter. Tresham is on his way now to warn Monteagle, and then Monteagle **7.** *(to write)* ______________ the letter for his own benefit. I'm not going to let it happen."

Johnson got down from his horse and slowly walked towards Fanshawe. "Peter, you can't do this, you know that. This is all in the past. It's done. It's been over for four hundred and fifty years. We know the truth now. Let's just let them get on with it and we can go home."

---

crazed [kreɪzd] wahnsinnig

"Stay away from me, Anthony. I've had long enough to think this through. I'm not going to allow him to betray Robin and the others and have them sent to their death."
As they continued to argue in the rain, Johnson heard the sound of **hooves** approaching and turned to see Catherine arriving on horseback. *What was she doing here? Had she been at the house? Had she followed him?*
As Johnson looked up at her, Catherine removed the gun from her **saddlebag** and addressed all three of the men together, although she never once took her eyes from Johnson.
"I never thought I would have to do something like this."
"Catherine, what is it? What's wrong? What are you talking about?"
"You can't murder all those innocent people, Anthony, no matter how bad things are. I can't stand by and watch you do it. Damn you for making me do this. *Damn you!*"
Fanshawe swung his gun around at Catherine. "Shut up, just shut up!"
Johnson stood speechless between them, wondering how things had deteriorated so quickly to the extent that these people he cared about were now pointing guns at each other. He saw tears beginning to **well up** in Catherine's eyes and slowly realized that there might be no resolution to this situation, no compromise that would allow all four of them to walk away. She finally shifted her gaze from Johnson to Fanshawe.
"I'm sorry, Peter, but I won't let you do this. I won't let you murder all those people. You'll have to kill me first."

---

hoof (*pl.* **hooves**) [hu:f / hu:vz] Huf **saddlebag** ['sædlbæg] Satteltasche **to well up** [ˌwel 'ʌp] aufsteigen

"Don't be stupid, Catherine. If you kill us, you will have to kill all the others as well, including your own husband. Doesn't it strike you as illogical to kill a large group of people in order to prevent us from killing another large group of people?"
But Catherine did not appear to be interested in debating the issue any further with Fanshawe or anybody else. The tears poured down her cheeks as she held the gun tightly and squeezed the **trigger**. The large flock of birds that had taken shelter from the storm in the trees overhead flew up as the gunpowder **ignited** with a bang, **propelling** the bullet through the air and straight into Fanshawe's chest. His eyes and mouth opened wide in shock as he dropped his own gun and slowly fell to the ground.
"Catherine, *no*!"
Johnson ran to Fanshawe and knelt beside him, too shocked to know what to do. As he turned to scream at Catherine, a second shot rang out. He suddenly felt a warm sensation spread throughout his chest as the noises around him began to sound **muffled**. He had lost all feeling in his legs, and slowly he slid to the ground beside Fanshawe. He opened his eyes and could just make out the shape of Catherine dismounting from her horse, dropping something from her hand, and falling to her knees beside him. She took off her cloak, folded it, and placed it under his head. As she leaned over him, a tear fell from her cheek onto his lower lip. A moment later he felt the warmth of her face pressing against his and heard her whisper, "You broke my heart."

---

trigger ['trɪgə] Abzug **to ignite** [ɪg'naɪt] sich entzünden **to propel** [prə'pel] antreiben **muffled** ['mʌfld] gedämpft

A single question flashed through his mind: *Am I really going to die?* He managed to keep his eyes open long enough to get a good look at her. She seemed older, and thinner, and tired. The colour had gone from her face and her eyes had lost the **sparkle** that **had** once so **captivated** him. He had to use his last seconds to make the most difficult decision of his life. If he told Catherine that he hadn't believed in the plot, that he had never really been a part of it, she would have to live with the guilt that she had unnecessarily killed the man she once loved. But this would also have suggested that he was indeed planning to betray Robin and the others; how would Catherine have been able to reconcile those two things? He couldn't burden her with that, but now that he was leaving her for the last time, he also didn't want her to think of him as a murderer. Was it better to leave a doubt in her mind, or to convince her that she had done the right thing by killing him? He wanted to tell her to make sure that Monteagle got the message so that history would resume its natural course, but this would **have sown** the seeds of confusion in Catherine's mind again, and in any event he was confident that Tresham would now succeed in telling Monteagle; history would play itself out exactly as it was supposed to. He wanted to tell her that the gunpowder beneath the House of Lords had decayed once again and that there was no risk of it exploding. In the end he lifted his left hand and held up the finger on which he wore Smith's silver ring. "Take this, please."

As she removed the ring from his finger, he looked at her

---

sparkle ['spɑːkl] Funkeln **to captivate** ['kæptɪveɪt] bezaubern
to sow (sowed, sown) [səʊ / səʊd / səʊn] säen

and managed a weak smile. "I love you, Catherine. I always did." Distraught and exhausted, Catherine lowered her head and cried. Johnson looked at her for as long as his eyes were able to focus; he held her hand as long as he was able to feel. The image of Catherine's face became fainter until it faded completely and he could no longer keep his eyelids from closing.

Epilogue

Johnson tumbled through the dark. All he felt was confusion and pain. Their mission had failed, they had failed, and it was his fault. He had been blinded by his own illusions, had only thought of Catherine, and hadn't seen what was going on in Fanshawe's mind. He could have stopped him, but he had been too involved in his own world to notice the signs. And there had been many signs that something was not right. This trip, this time-travel, had been the chance of a lifetime, and he had wasted it. All he had done was fool around, breaking hearts and destroying lives. The shots had wounded him terribly, and not just him, but Fanshawe, too. There was no way that both of them would be able to survive the two months they still had to stay in the past before they could return to their own time and their old lives. They would die here, in the past, and he would never be able to share the things he had seen. He so much wanted to tell everything, to pass on his experience. He wanted to tell of the *people*, the real people, who had lived and breathed and loved and dreamed. He wanted people in his own time to understand that history was always the result of the actions, desires, feelings of human beings. Places and dates were just the cornerstones, they didn't really matter. It was the people who mattered, people who lived dozens and hundreds of years ago, people who were long gone, but who would always be at the centre of history.

As he was following these thoughts, which were slowly becoming more settled and focussed, he realized that the most important lesson he and Fanshawe had learned was that people hadn't changed much over the centuries. They were basically the same hundreds of years ago as they were in his time. They had always been and still were guided by the same basic values: faith, friendship, and love. And those were also the reasons for his own failure, and Fanshawe's, and probably also the plotters'. If all we did was done for friendship, love, and faith, he thought, then maybe the failure wasn't all that disastrous. Maybe those reasons are more important than the result.

Suddenly, a voice interrupted his thoughts. "Professor! My God, Professor! Fanshawe! Hurry – fetch a doctor!"
And slowly he opened his eyes.
He saw Fanshawe lying beside him, breathing softly in the blue light of the Department's neon lamps. Smith's face hovered above him.
"What …?" he croaked. "Are we …? How …?"
"Tresham." It was Fanshawe's voice. "Tresham betrayed them. But he was not the only one. We didn't save them." His voice faded.
"We already know about Tresham, Fanshawe. But what about the doctors? That was you, am I right? You are the two doctors!" Smith was breathless with excitement. "We

always knew it was true, it couldn't just have been pure chance that those doctors, the ones the plotters talked about, were never found. Two mysterious doctors called Johnson and Fanshawe! It was you, wasn't it?"

"It was …?", Johnson and Fanshawe echoed simultaneously.

"The two doctors we sent you to search for," insisted Smith. "What happened? Who informed Catherine Catesby and let her warn the others? Who …?"

Once again, Johnson's mind began to race and he sat up slowly, looking first at Fanshawe, then back at Smith. Doctors? Smith never has mentioned any doctors! The others? Who had Catherine warned? Monteagle? Surely not Robin? But perhaps he would have finally believed her, once Fanshawe and Johnson had disappeard … Had they indeed changed the course of history? "May I have a history book on the Gunpowder Plot?" he asked slowly.

Smith gave him an astonished look, then handed him what he had asked for. He skipped through the pages and when he found the passage he was looking for, he started reading aloud:

The fifteen coup plotters – *fifteen! not thirteen!* – had intended to blow up the House of Lords on the day that Parliament convened, killing the king in the process. Guy Fawkes, who had fought for Spain as a mercenary, would light the fuse and then flee to Spain, while Robert Catesby, the leader of the plot, would raise a rebellion among Catholics in the north of England. Catesby's wife, a Protestant, is thought to have warned him in advance that the Plot had been discovered. If this is true, however, it is unclear why he did not believe her. One of the greatest mysteries of the

Gunpowder Plot concerns two doctors from the North. They were said to have belonged to the core group of plotters, but vanished into thin air just before it failed ..."

"But –" Fanshawe gasped, "but that's not true! That's not what happened! That isn't the truth! What became of the plotters, Smith? Did the plot fail?"
Johnson closed the book slowly, a little smile on his lips. "Truth is the daughter of Time", he murmured, "and Time will tell."

Historical Note

Catherine Catesby (née Leigh), wife of Robert Catesby, died in 1597. She has been used here purely for dramatic purposes. All the other characters (with the obvious exceptions of Anthony Johnson, Peter Fanshawe, and Mrs Smith) as well as events and dates are as accurate as possible. However, certain facts surrounding the plot remain disputed. Two in particular are worth highlighting here. First, there is no evidence that the plotters originally planned to dig a tunnel under the Houses of Parliament. In the trial that followed the capture of eight of the men, the **prosecution** claimed that the plotters attempted to dig the tunnel between 11th December 1604 and 25th March 1605, but gave up when it became impractical due to the thickness of the walls. Historians believe that the idea of a tunnel worked to the advantage of the prosecution as it held a special **sinister** element that would add to the evil image of the men which they

---

prosecution [ˌprɒsɪˈkjuːʃn] Anklage **sinister** [ˈsɪnɪstə] unheilvoll

wished to portray. Second, although for most historians the Monteagle letter is the key to the failure of the plot, its author and origins are still unknown. That Francis Tresham informed Lord Monteagle, either orally or in writing, remains speculation.

Further Reading

Fraser, Antonia, *The Gunpowder Plot:* Terror and Faith in 1605, Phoenix, 2002
Haynes, Alan, *The Gunpowder Plot*, Sutton Publishing, 2005
Hogge, Alice, *God's Secret Agents:* Queen Elizabeth's Forbidden Priests and the Hatching of the Gunpowder Plot, HarperCollins, 2005
Travers, James, *Gunpowder: The Players Behind the Plot*, The National Archives, 2005

Solutions

Exercise 1
1. True, 2. False, 3. False, 4. True, 5. False, 6. False, 7. True, 8. False, 9. True, 10. False

Exercise 2
1g, 2c, 3a, 4d, 5f, 6h, 7e, 8b

Exercise 3
1d, 2j, 3e, 4g, 5a, 6i, 7h, 8f, 9b, 10c

Exercise 4
1. Time-travel is limited by the laws of physics.
2. Some of the paradoxes haven't been resolved yet.
3. Is the past overruled by the future?
4. Some mice were injected with poison. (or: Poison was injected into some mice.)
5. Guy Fawkes was caught.
6. You will be trained in emotional detachment.
7. The plot was uncovered (by Lord Monteagle).
8. The Catholics were punished.
9. Your judgement could be impaired.
10. The entire process must be studied.

Exercise 5
1. chill, 2. cast, 3. came, 4. collective, 5. coming, 6. candle, 7. centre, 8. committed, 9. crucial, 10. Catesby

Exercise 6
1d, 2a, 3b, 4a, 5d, 6a

Exercise 7

1. desperately, 2. hard, 3. bad, 4. rapid, 5. vigorous, 6. visible, 7. cool, 8. convincingly; well

Exercise 8

1, 4, 5, 7

Exercise 9

1. realized/were standing, 2. were holding/arrived, 3. was yawning/entered, 4. spotted/was smiling, 5. realized/was taking, 6. occurred/were digging, 7. was carrying/arrived, 8. was sitting/heard

Exercise 10

1c, 2d, 3f, 4a, 5g, 6b, 7h, 8e

Exercise 11

1. The plotters wouldn't have needed a different strategy if the tunnel hadn't flooded.
2. If Fanshawe had remained emotionally detached, he wouldn't have told the plotters about the cellars.
3. Fanshawe and Johnson wouldn't have had an opportunity to infiltrate the group if Catesby's son hadn't fallen ill.
4. If Johnson hadn't been a famous historian, he wouldn't have been asked to travel back to the seventeenth century.
5. If Johnson's mother hadn't died tragically, he wouldn't have vowed never to love anybody again.
6. The British government wouldn't have established the Department of Historical Truth if the British hadn't lost the Taiwan War.

Exercise 12
1. gardens, 2. practice, 3. story, 4. guilt, 5. lie, 6. truth, 7. personality, 8. time, 9. sound, 10. Space

Exercise 13
1c, 2e, 3b, 4f, 5a, 6d

Exercise 14
1. thirty, 2. three, fifty, 3. theoretically, 4. taken off, 5. sell, 6. discreetly, 7. Catesby's, 8. Fawkes

Exercise 15
1. have been, 2. be (or have been), are (or were), 3. wouldn't be, 4. was, 5. were, 6. had been

Exercise 16
1b, 2d, 3c, 4b, 5c, 6a

Exercise 17
1. for, 2. of, 3. from, 4. With, 5. out of, 6. through, 7. in, 8. about, 9. for

Exercise 18
1. hatred, 2. truth, 3. arrival, 4. intolerance, 5. tension, 6. persecution, 7. persuasion, 8. loyalty, 9. commitment, 10. rebellion (or rebel)

Exercise 19
1d, 2g, 3h, 4e, 5a, 6b, 7c, 8f

Exercise 20
1d, 2e, 3a, 4h, 5i, 6b, 7g, 8c, 9f

Exercise 21

1g, 2d, 3f, 4c, 5a, 6b, 7e

Exercise 22

1. blind, 2. consumed, 3. attention, 4. guilty, 5. having, 6. even, 7. door, 8. face, 9. idiocy

Exercise 23

1c (gunpowder), 2d (tunnel), 3e (Catholics), 4a (barrel), 5b (letter)

Exercise 24

1. over, 2. off, 3. in, 4. out, 5. down, 6. up, 7. up

Exercise 25

1. further, trickier, 2. longer, more sympathetic, 3. closer, more uncomfortable, 4. more intelligent, better, 5. louder, worse

Exercise 26

1. shouted, 2. are you doing, 3. Have you lost, 4. have been, 5. saw, 6. were, 7. will write

Liebe Leserinnen und Leser,

Die einzelnen Titel aus der Reihe Lernschmöker sind den sechs verschiedenen Niveaustufen des Gemeinsamen Europäischen Referenzrahmens für Sprachen zugeordnet. Welcher Niveaustufe dieser Titel angehört, können Sie der Angabe auf dem Cover bzw. Buchrücken entnehmen.
Die Niveaustufen bedeuten:
A1/A2: *Elementare Sprachverwendung*, d.h.
A1: Sie können Einzelwörter und ganz einfache Sätze verstehen.
A2: Sie können ganz kurze und einfache Alltagstexte lesen.
B1/B2: *Selbständige Sprachverwendung*, d.h.
B1: Sie verstehen Texte, in denen v.a. sehr gebräuchliche Alltags- und Berufssprache vorkommt.
B2: Sie verstehen zeitgenössische literarische Prosatexte.
C1/C2: *Kompetente Sprachverwendung*, d.h.
C1: Sie verstehen Sachtexte, technische Fachartikel sowie literarische Texte
C2: Sie verstehen jede Art geschriebener Texte, auch wenn sie inhaltlich und sprachlich komplex sind.

Sollten Sie ganz genau wissen wollen, welche Niveaustufe für Sie geeignet ist, so finden Sie auf unserer Website unter www.langenscheidt.de sowohl eine kompakte Beschreibung der einzelnen Referenzniveaus als auch eine Orientierungshilfe zur Selbstbeurteilung in Bezug auf die verschiedenen Niveaustufen.
So finden Sie die Lektüre, die ideal auf Ihre Sprachkenntnisse und Bedürfnisse zugeschnitten ist.
Viel Spaß beim Lernschmökern!

Ihre Langenscheidt Redaktion